First published by MrsDBooks LLC

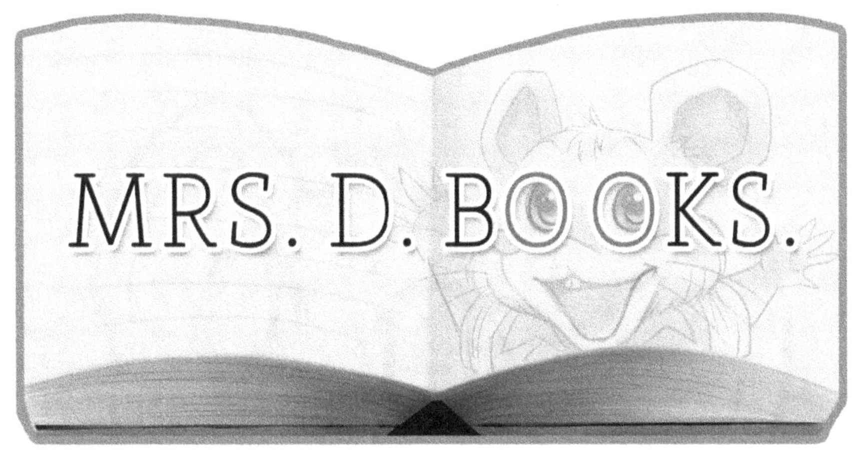

ISBN:978-1725979437

This book is a work of fiction. Places, events, and situations in this book
are purely fictional, and any resemblance to actual persons, living or
dead, is coincidental.

To order additional paperback or
hardcover copies of this book, please visit
Amazon.com, Barnesandnoble.com, or
the author's website, www.mrsdbooks.net, or
email olga@mrsdbooks.com

E-book versions are also available through
Amazon, Barnes and Noble,
and Apple.

CARLO THE MOUSE:

Coloring & Activity Kids Book 2

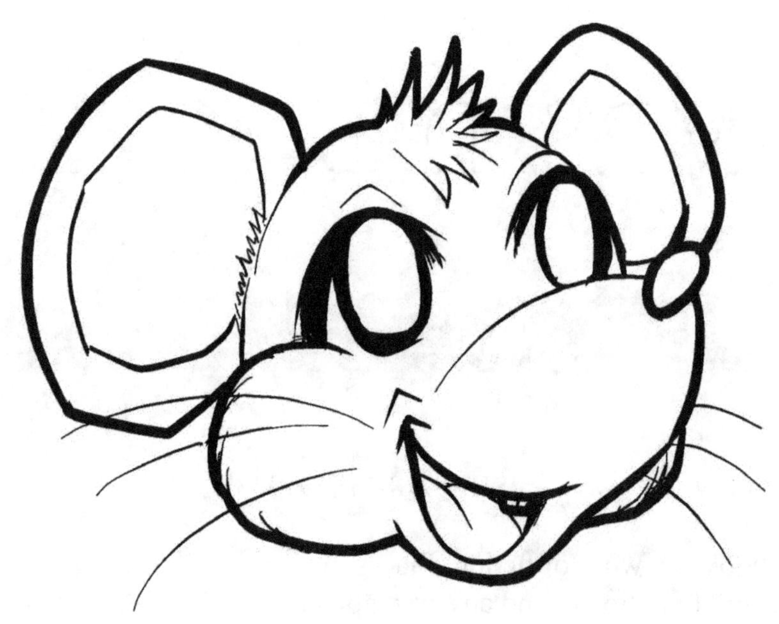

By

MRS. D.

Illustrated by Chanoa

How Carlo the Mouse Took the World by the Horns

George Bernard Shaw once said, "Make it a rule never to give a child a book you would not read yourself." Writing my first book, *Carlo the Mouse on Vacation*, I kept his advice in mind. I wanted to create a children's book that would appeal not only to children but to grown-ups as well. I hoped my story would attract a wider sector of readers of different ages and bring back memories of youthful fun and good laughs. Taking into consideration the fact that grown-ups are the ones who introduce books to children, I tried to lift the bar so the storyline would appeal to older readers too. If necessary, they could easily explain the story to the children if they were too young to understand it.

This decision slightly raised the eyebrows of some cynical folks. Thank heavens it did not bother the young fans. They fell in love with the daring mouse as soon as they saw the happy Carlo beaming from the cover of this book. Since the day I introduced this adventurous mouse to readers, he has managed to find many good friends around the globe. Readers like how Carlo took the world by the horns. I have received emails, messages, suggestions, pictures, and even some stories about Carlo's future adventures, which I may use when the time is right.

Anyone who has read *Carlo the Mouse on Vacation* might remember that the story finished with Carlo sitting inside an empty pizza box. We'll let him sit there for a while and think of how he will outsmart the man in black. Meanwhile, I will tell you the story that led to the series of six books on Carlo the mouse as a baby.

It was the day of my daughter's bridal shower. Before the girls hit the town to have fun, I volunteered to babysit for their children. The children happened to be very young, between 3 and 7 years old, and it was very challenging to entertain them all afternoon. Tired of chasing them around, I pulled out a box with books and started showing them colorful illustrations from my first book, *Carlo the Mouse on Vacation*. Before I knew it, the kids showered me with many questions about the Florida mouse. Who does not know about that famous mouse! But I stumbled on the famous cook, who yelled "Baaam" from the TV and scared babies in the delivery room.

The kids were so excited to find out what Carlo did inside the hospital that I started cooking up new stories about Carlo as a baby. There were many questions about the doctors, the hospital staff, and Carlo's mom and dad. As they looked at the colorful illustrations, the kids were coming up with so many ideas that my head began to spin. To calm them down, I came up with stories of how Carlo caused trouble inside the hospital. Their interest sparked immediately.

At first, the kids wanted Carlo to do bad things and act silly, but I thought it would be more fun if we established some rules, which, of course, Carlo would eventually break and get himself in more trouble. In this way, younger children would learn something useful from his adventures while still having fun. I spent a lot of time in the hospital with my sick father and had a good idea of how a nosy mouse could get in trouble. Jumping in front of each other in their excitement, the children came up with many rules and some good propositions.

It was already close to dinnertime, but the game was

not even close to an end. That was when my husband came to the rescue. He found a few flashlights and started the real adventures. Armed with flashlights and plastic bags, the young hunters started searching all the closets in the house. While their mission was going on, I managed to cook meatballs and spaghetti. Looking for clues that Carlo left in the closet, my husband finally lured the children to the kitchen so we could feed them. Who could refuse Mrs. D's meatballs and spaghetti, which Carlo did not manage to taste when he tried to visit Mrs. D's kitchen? In no time, the plates were empty and the children went back to searching for the sneaky mouse until they could not keep their eyes open. In the middle of the night, I could still hear them talking about the little mouse causing trouble in the hospital.

The next day, I received calls from their parents asking me the name of the book I had read to their children, because they were still looking for some mouse that was hiding in their closet.

"Unwritten book," I said. At that moment, I knew I must go back in time and write new stories about Carlo the mouse, beginning the day he was born. The game the children created that summer did not stop and is going on to this day. It became more interesting when we started working on illustrations and I could show my little friends how the stories were coming to life. Now the game is more intriguing, because they can visualize the scenes from the illustrations and still have an opportunity to come up with their own stories. Carlo the Mouse, Coloring Book 2 includes fun sketches from books 4, 5 and 6. It is perfect for coloring with colored pencils or whatever you choose. Coloring is relaxing activity, which will sending you on a creative adventure. So spark your creativity and unleash your inner artist with Carlo the Mouse coloring books!

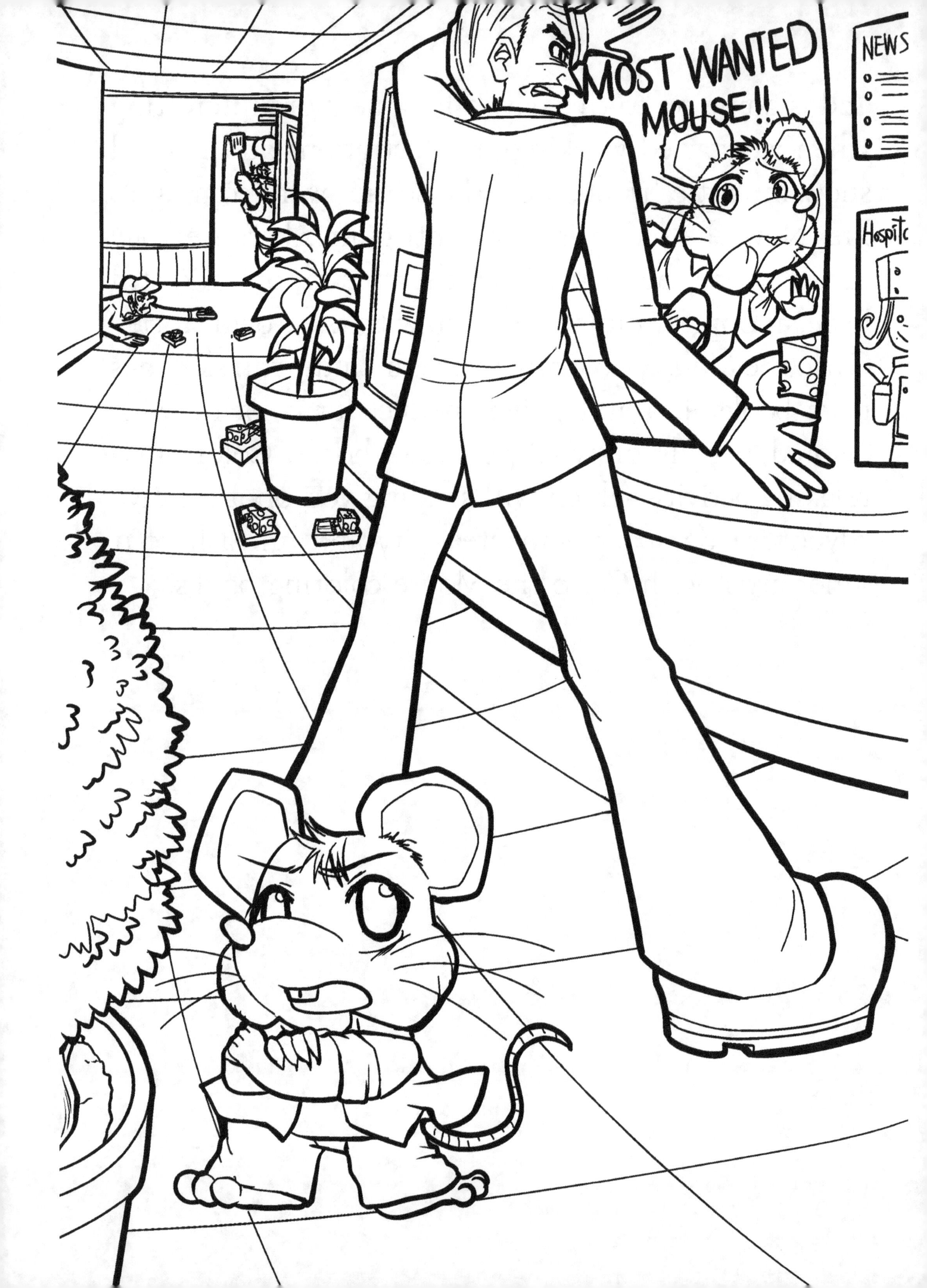
MOST WANTED
MOUSE!!
NEWS
Hospita

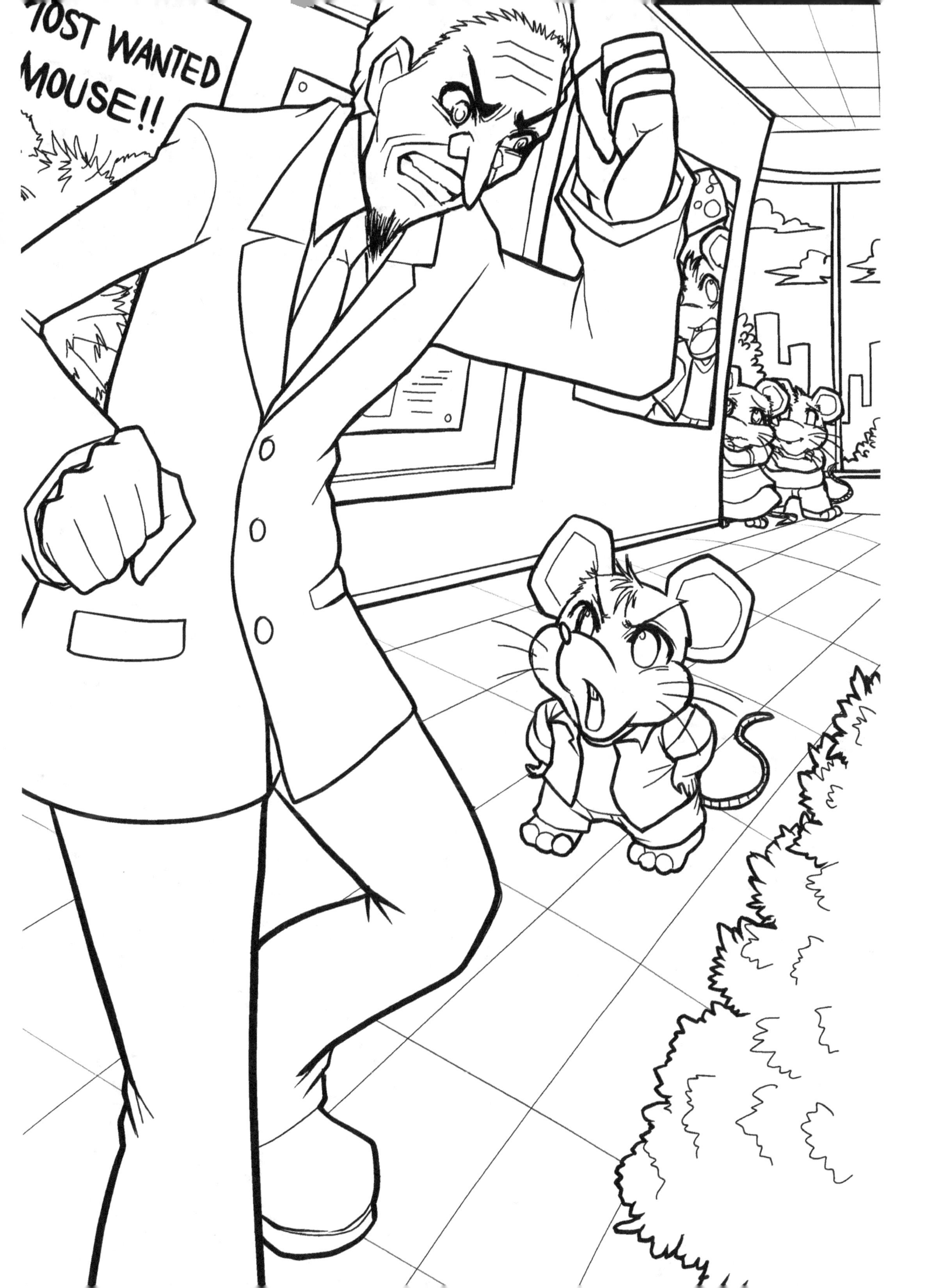

MOST WANTED
MOUSE!!

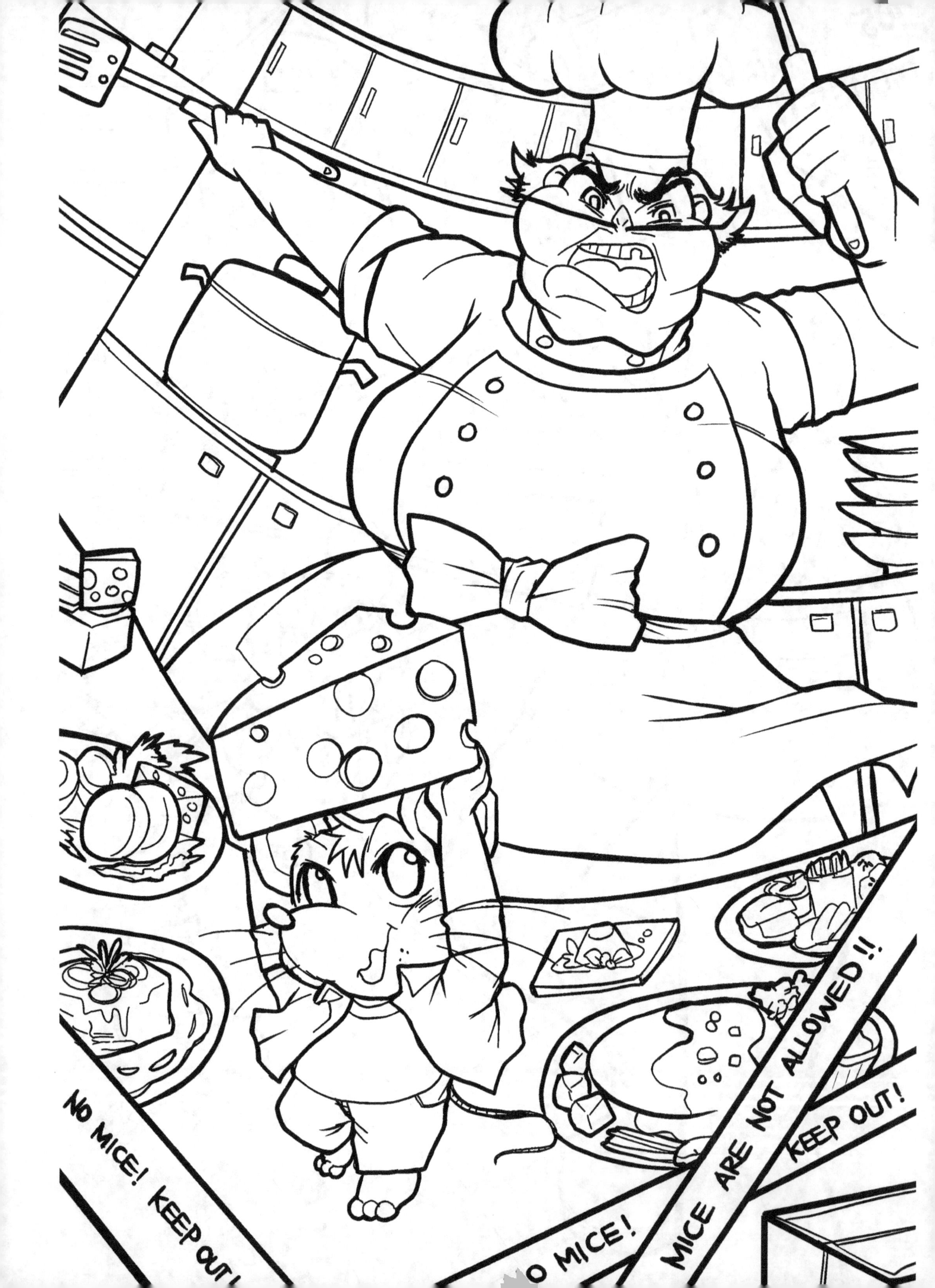

NO MICE! KEEP OUT!
O MICE!
MICE ARE NOT ALLOWED !!
KEEP OUT!

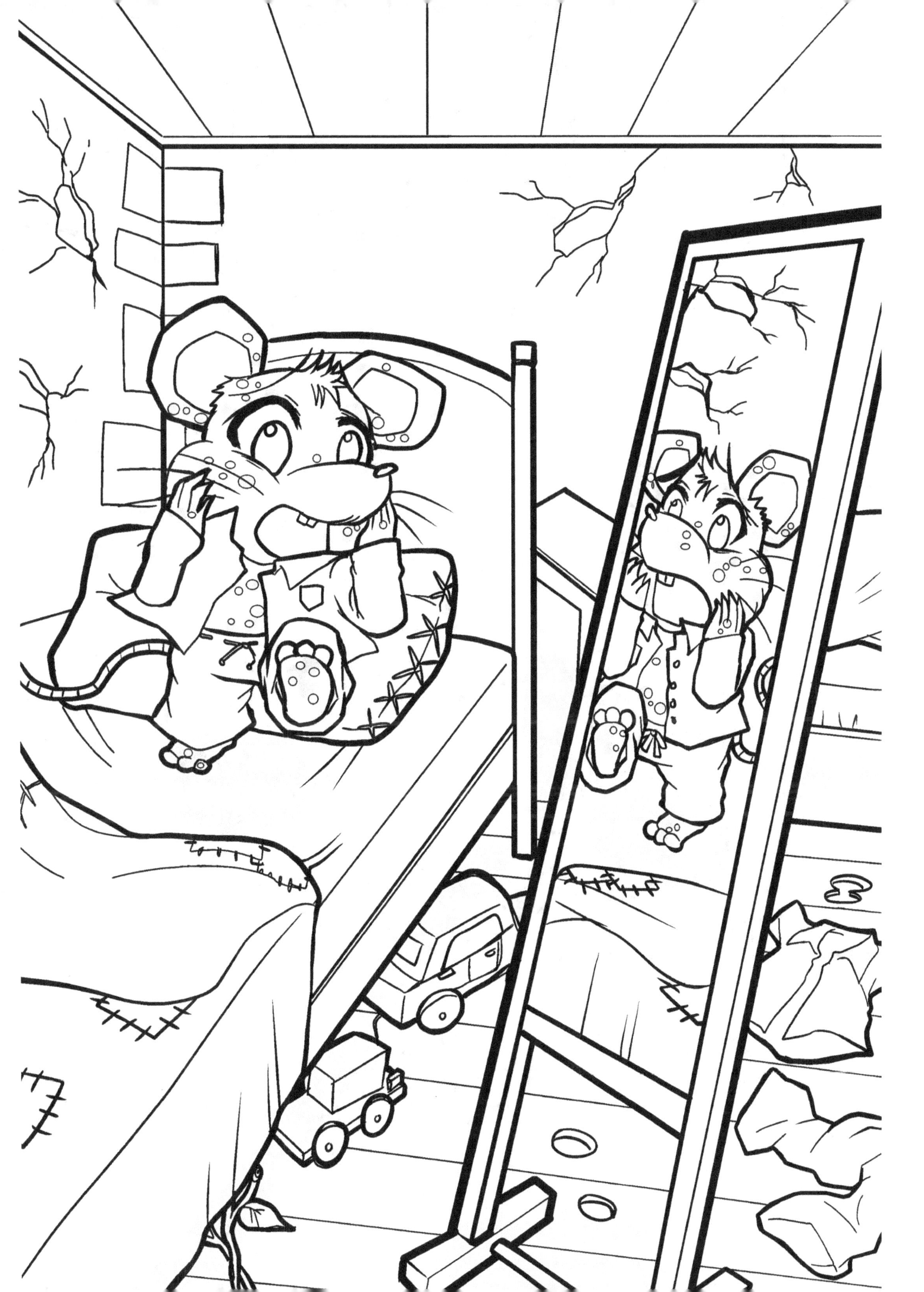

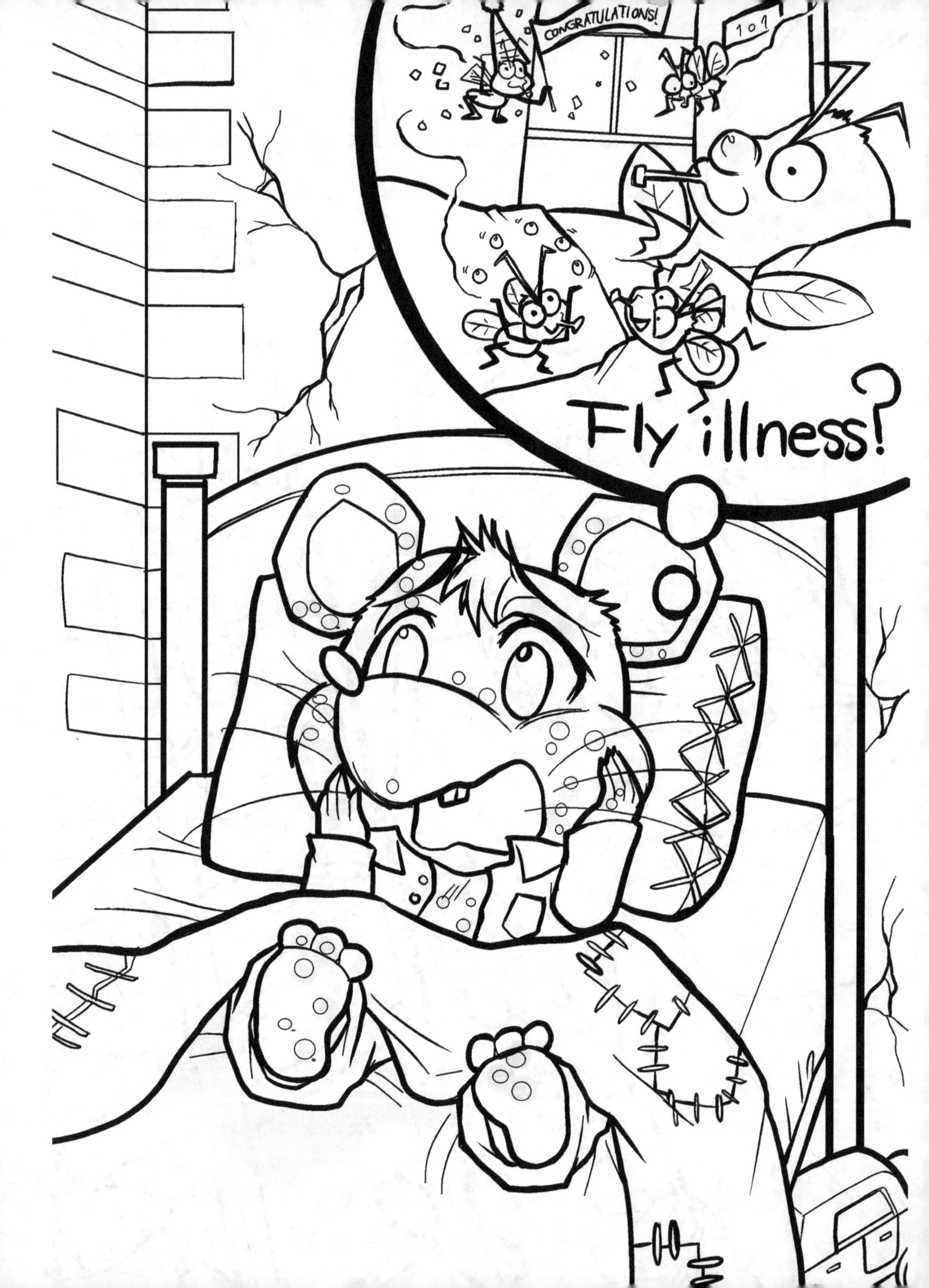

CONGRATULATIONS!
Fly illness?

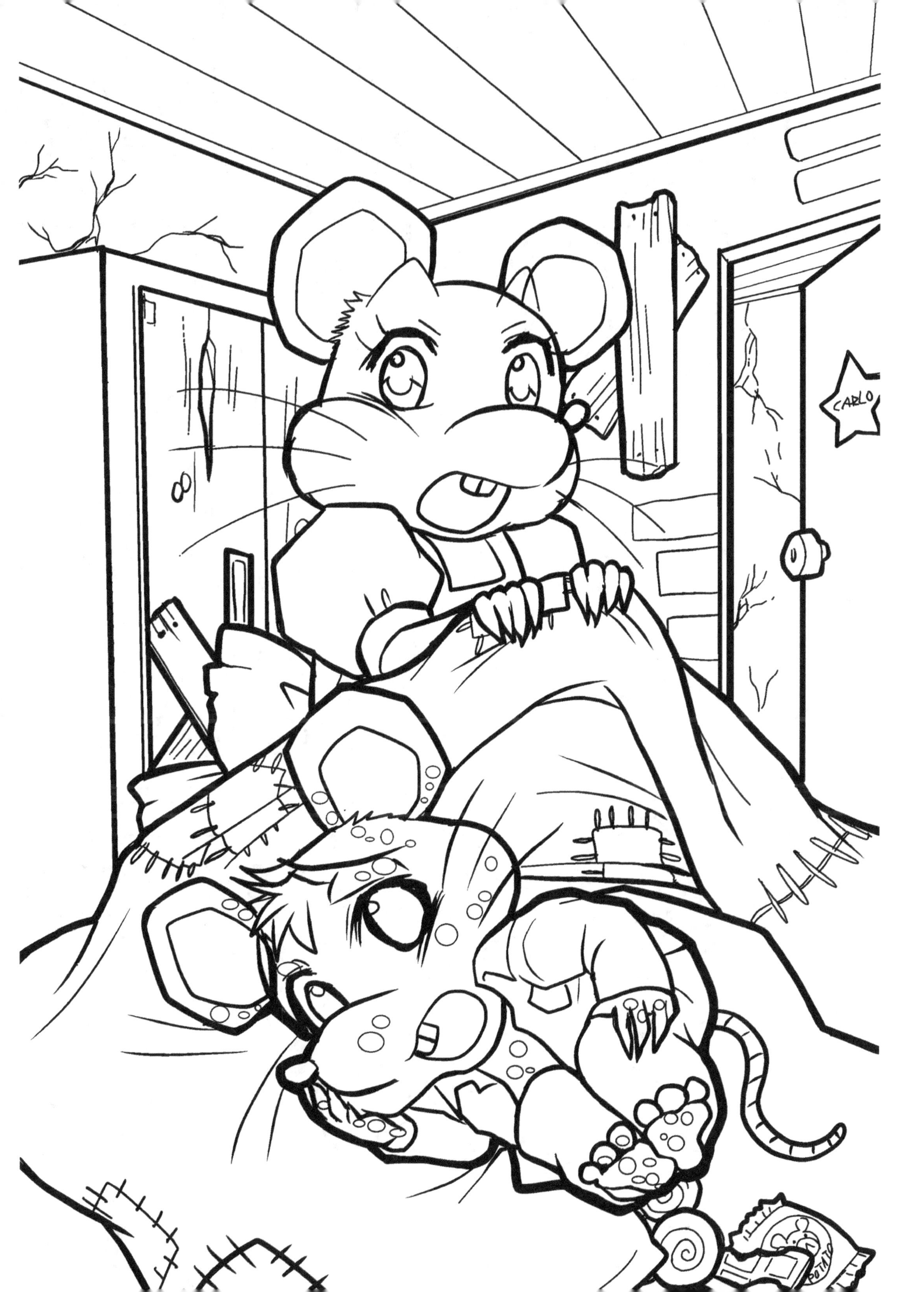
CARLO
POTATO

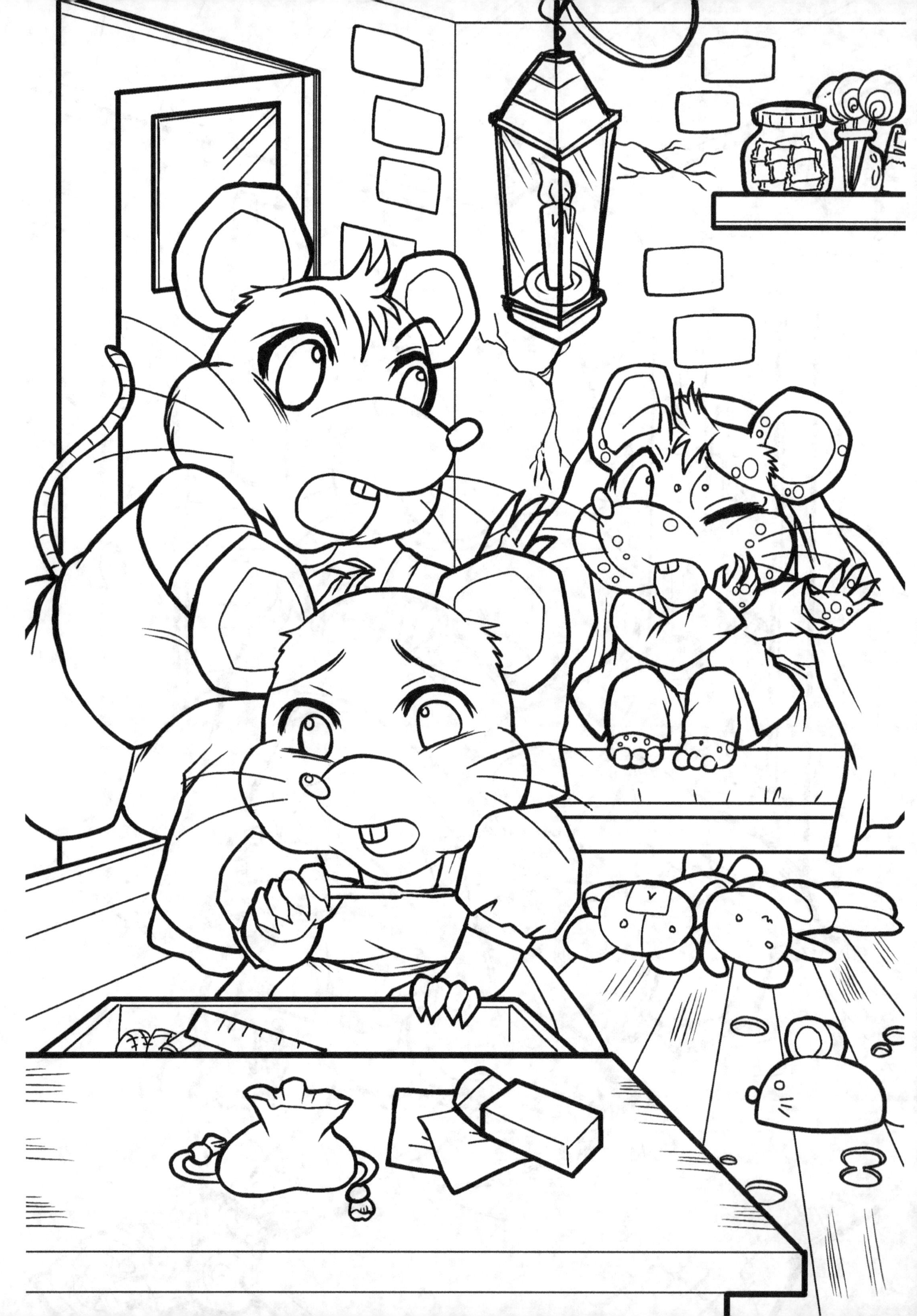

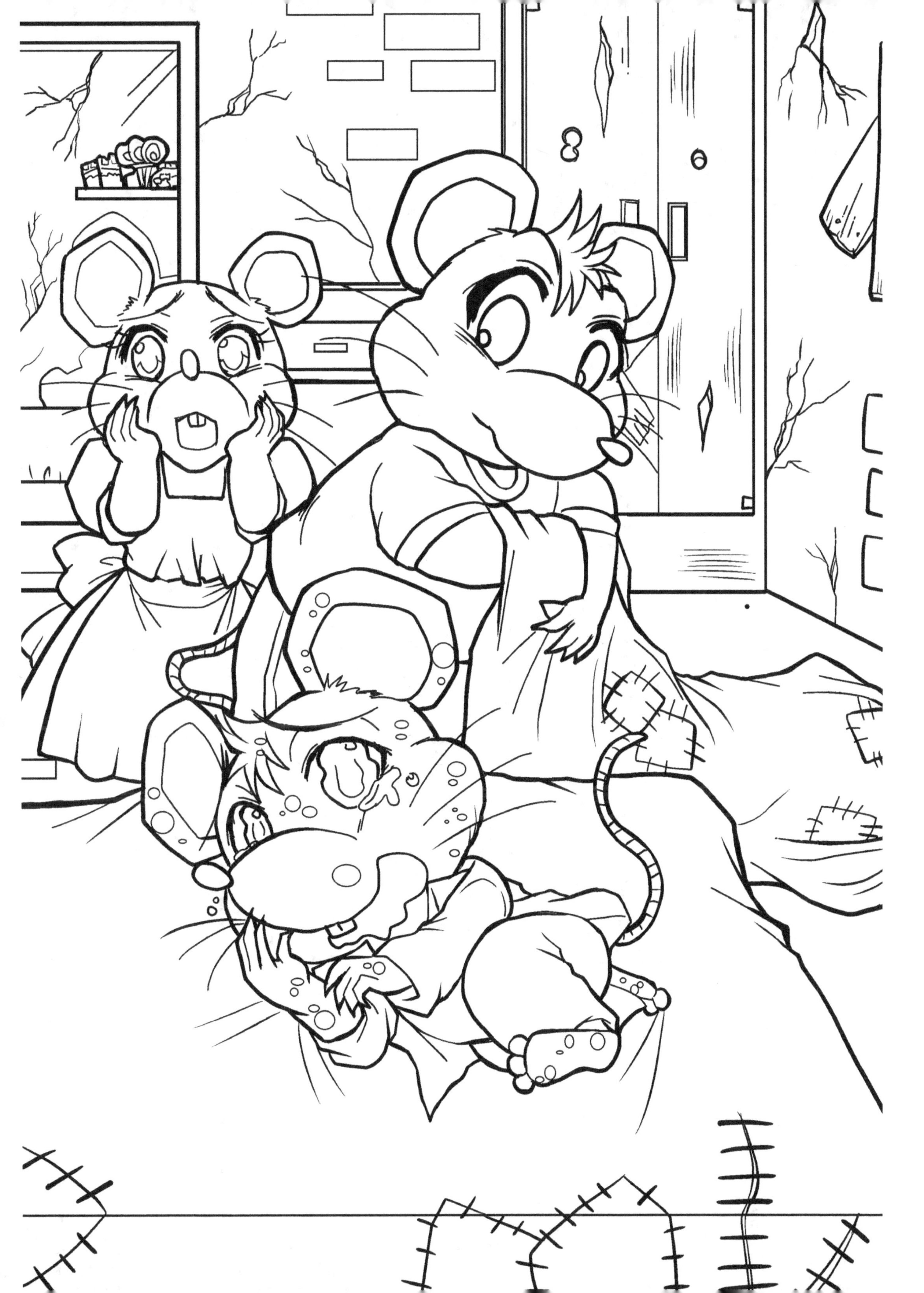

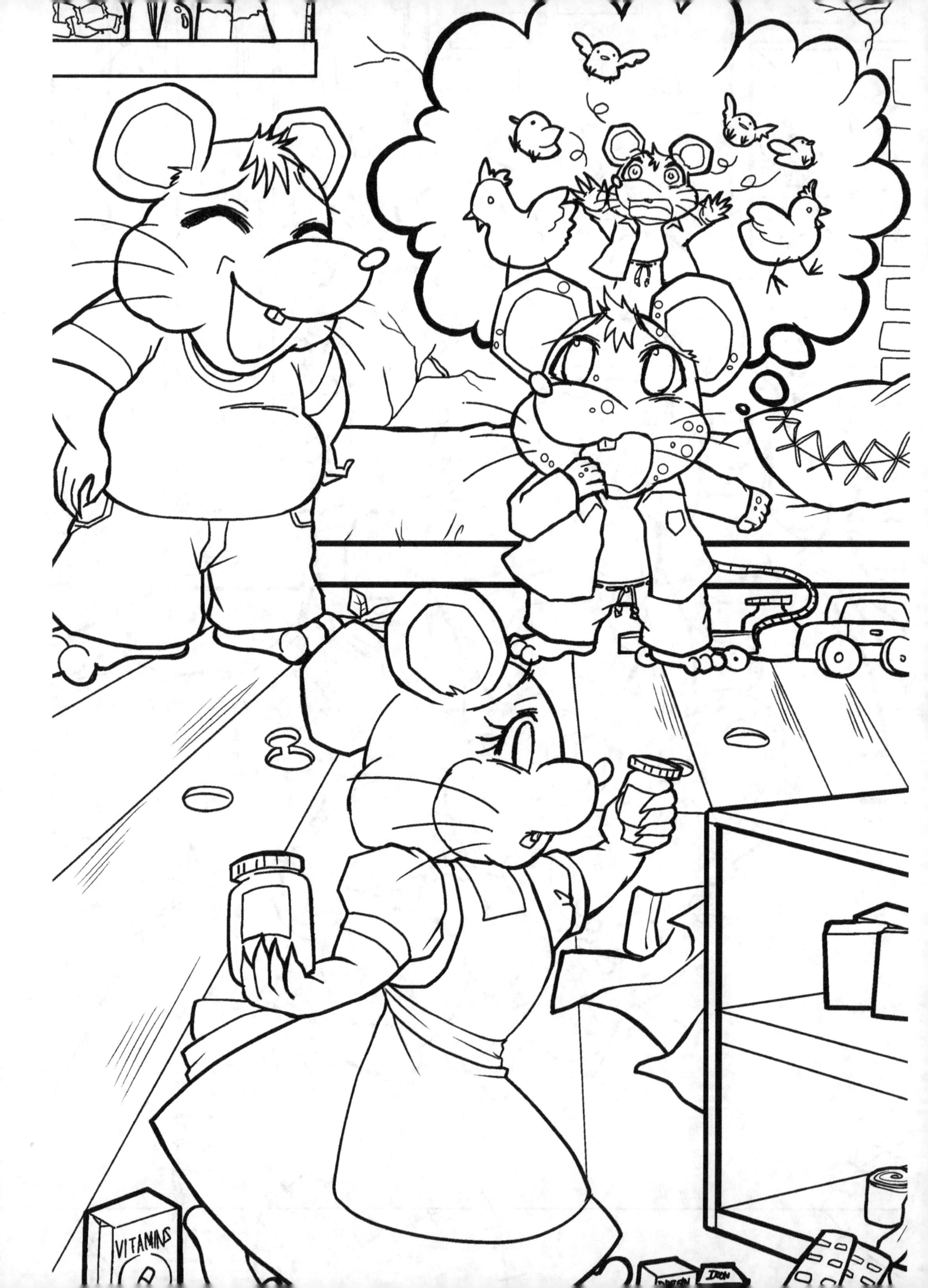
VITAMINS

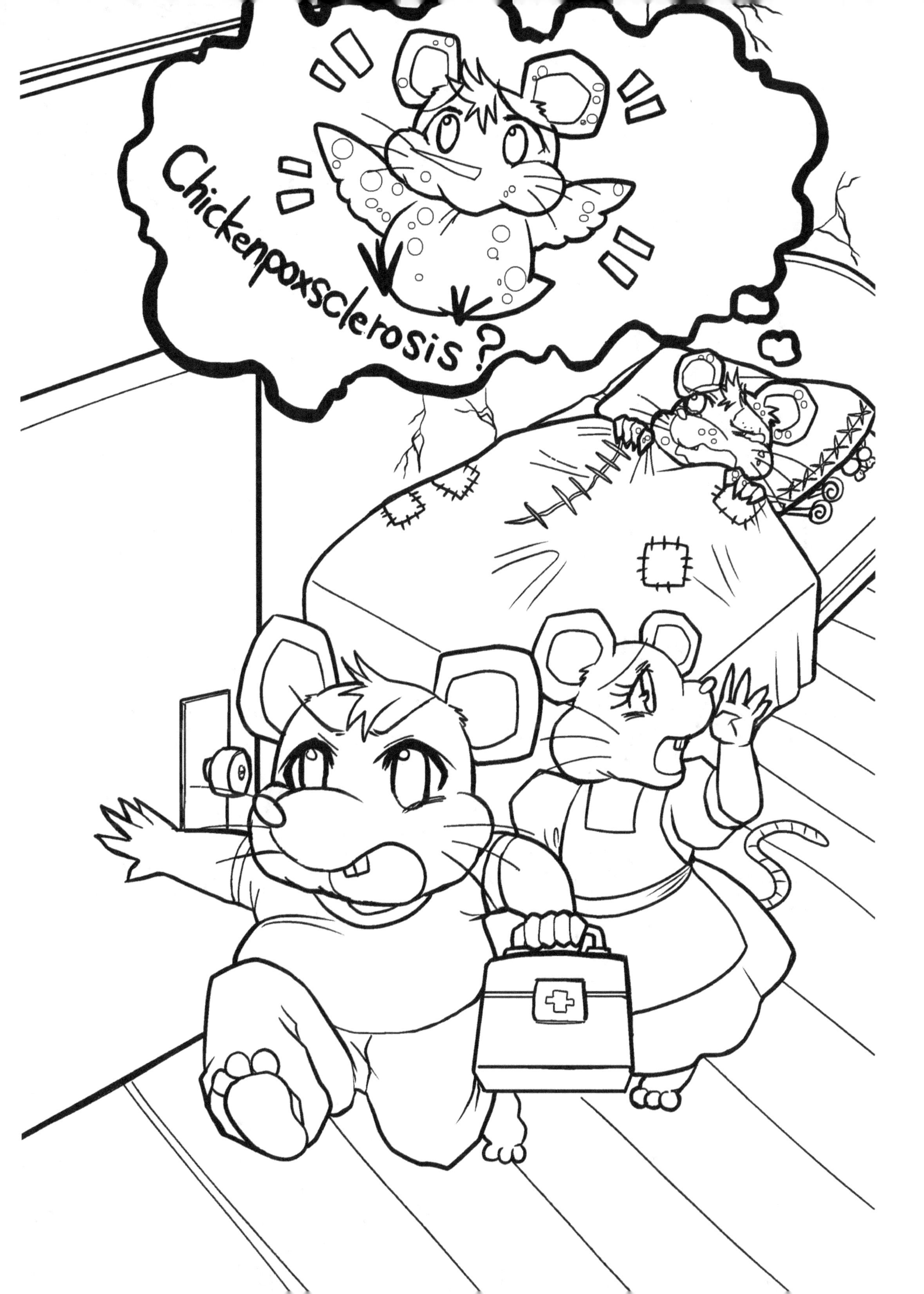

Chickenpoxsclerosis?

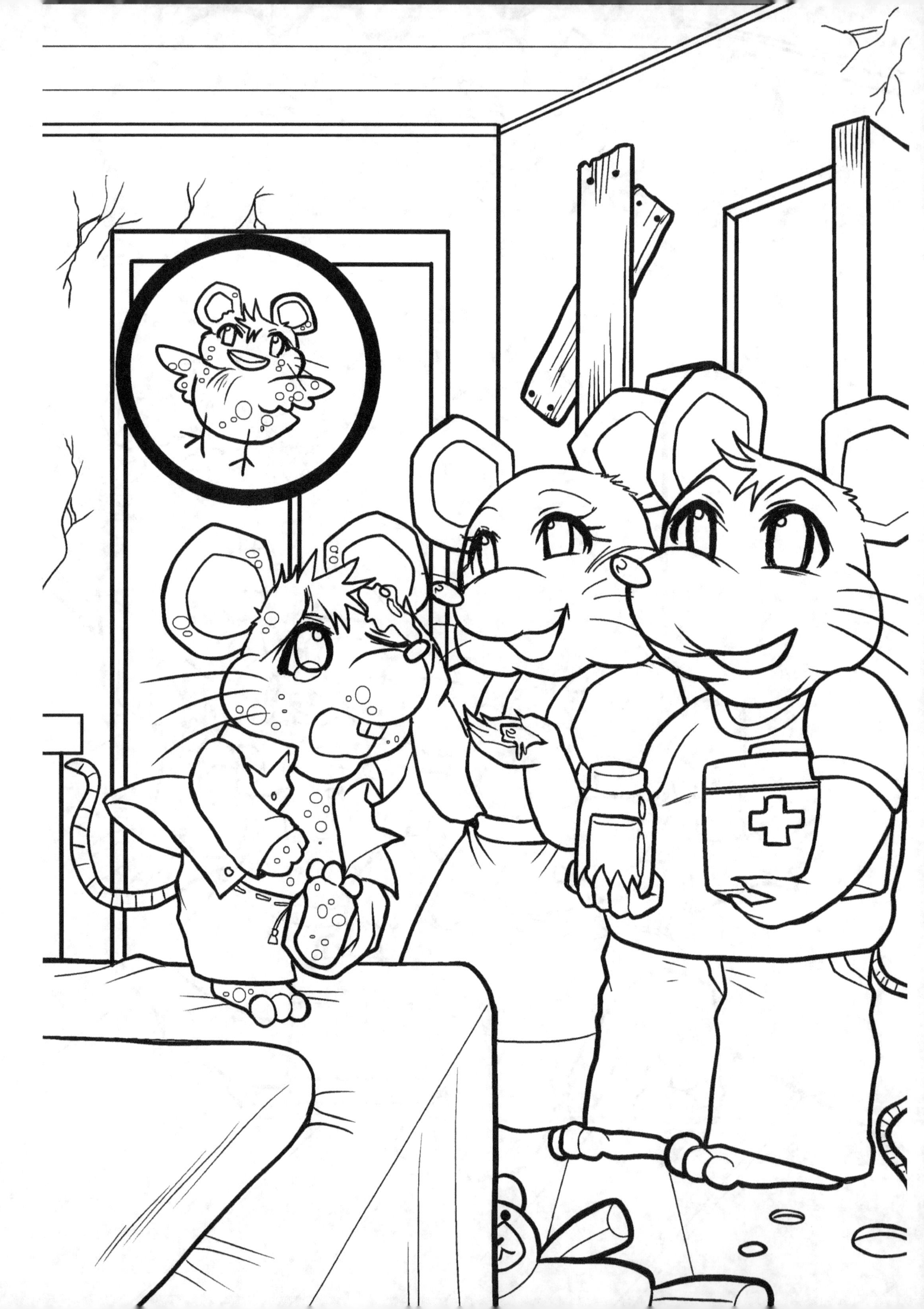

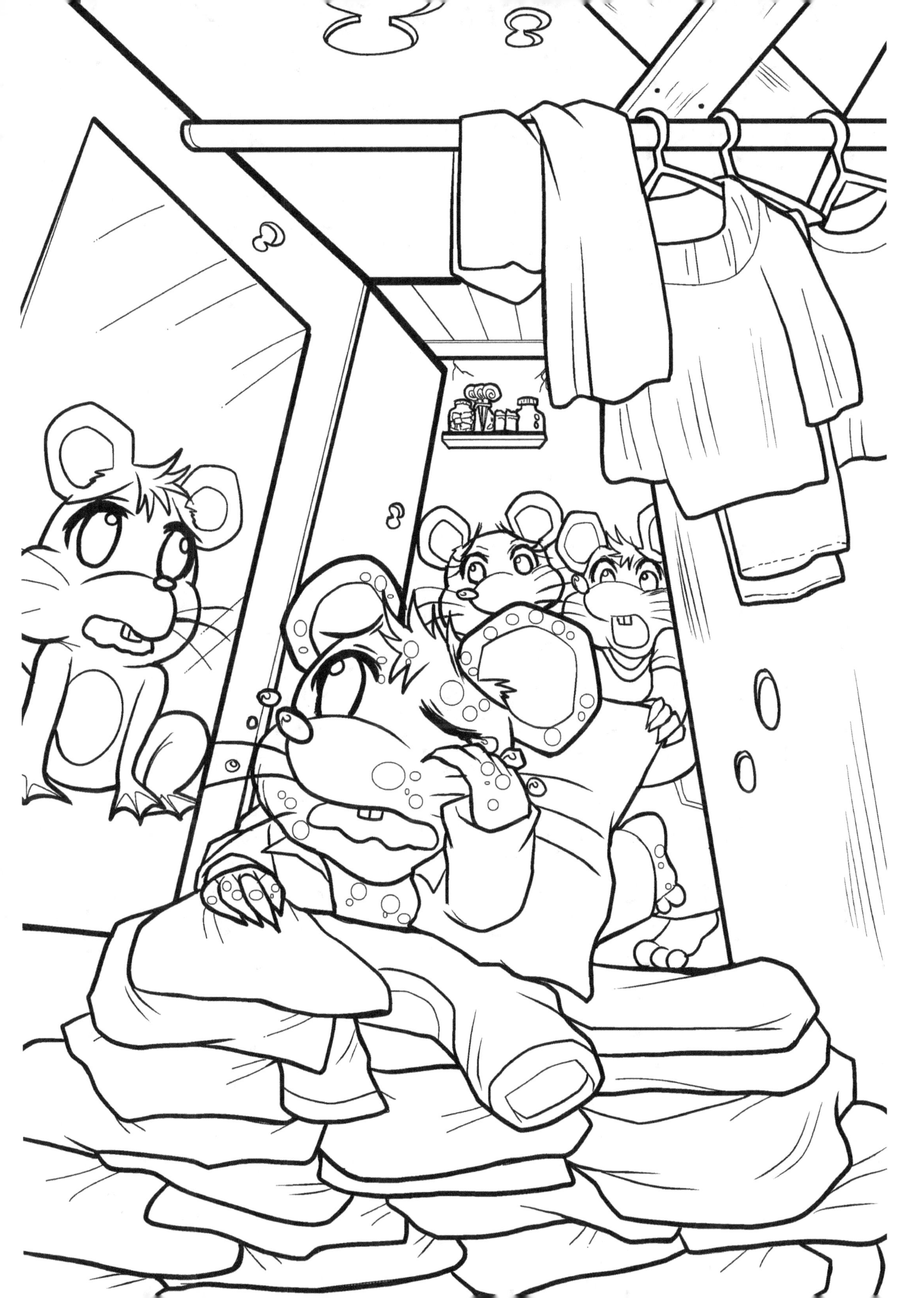

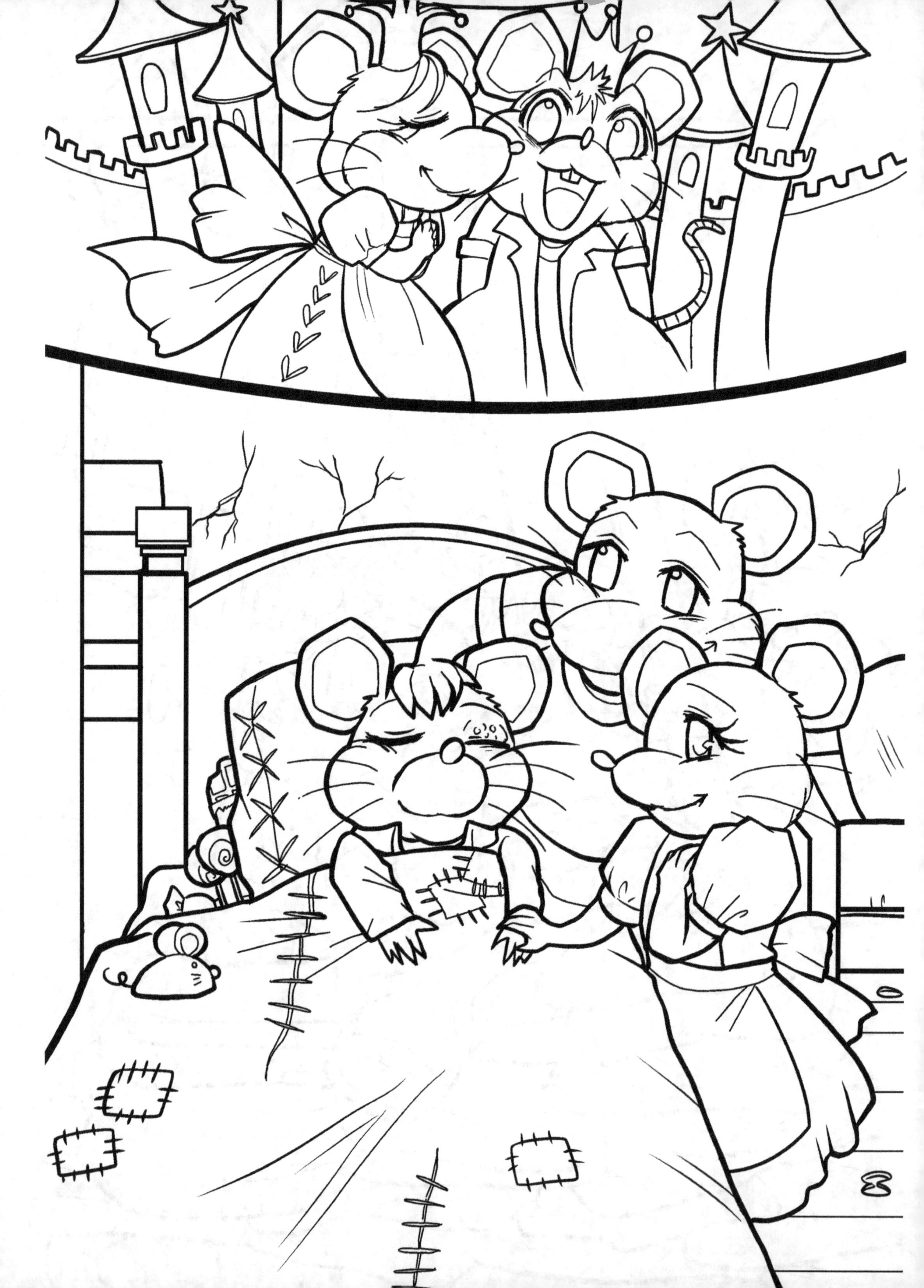

Put the Letters in Order!

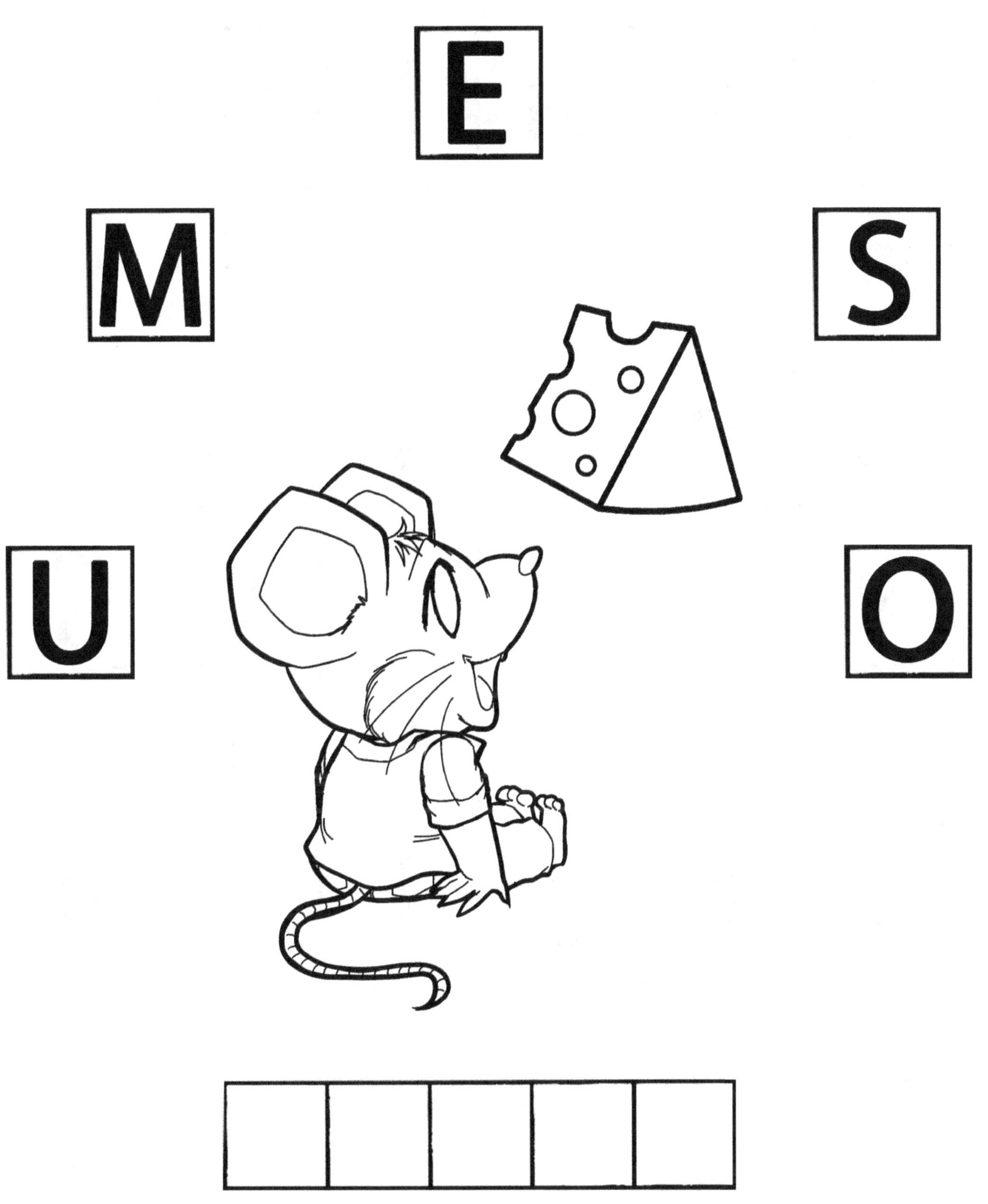

Look for the subjects!

z	f	a	t	h	f
m	l	n	u	j	r
S	o	t	l	n	x
v	w	r	i	c	g
b	e	e	p	k	y
q	r	a	i	n	d

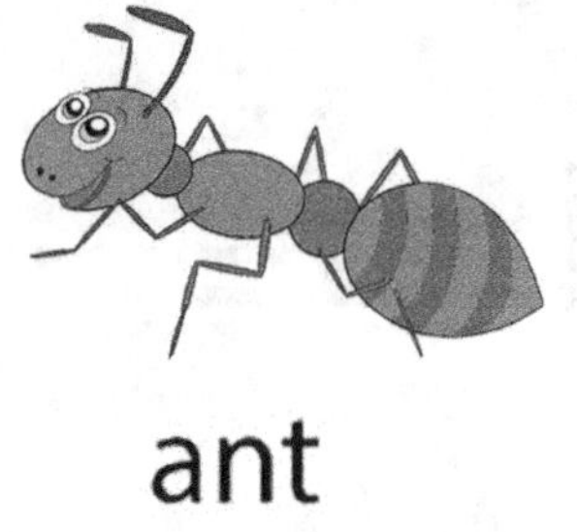

ant

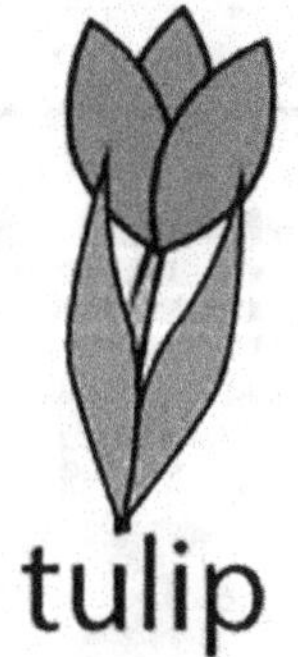

tulip

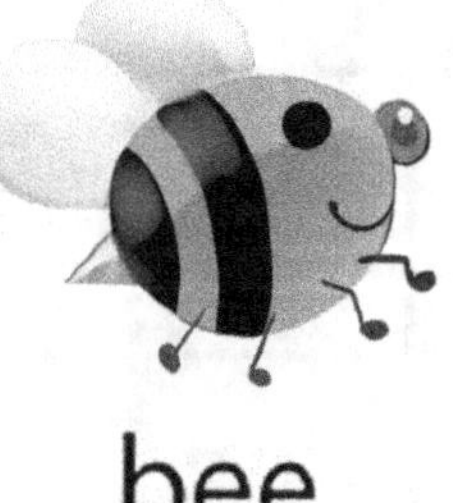

bee

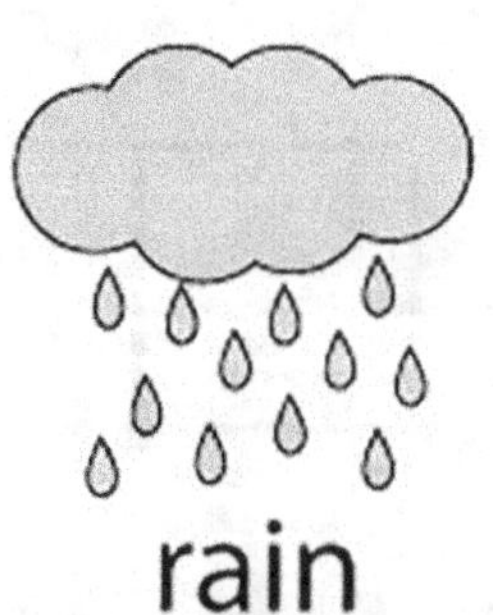

rain

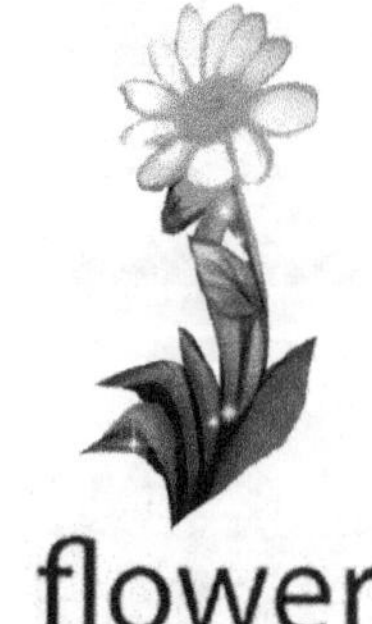

flower

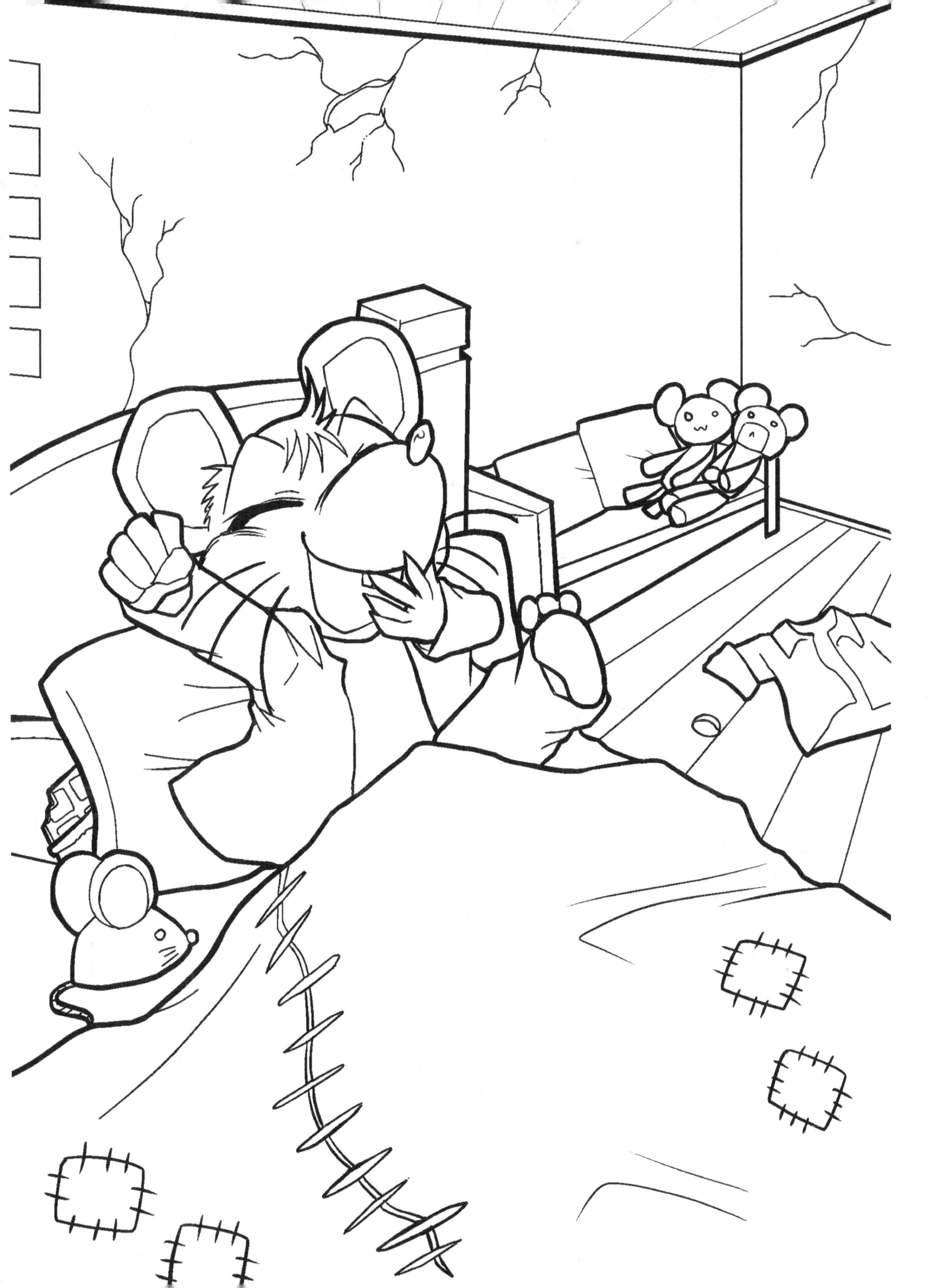

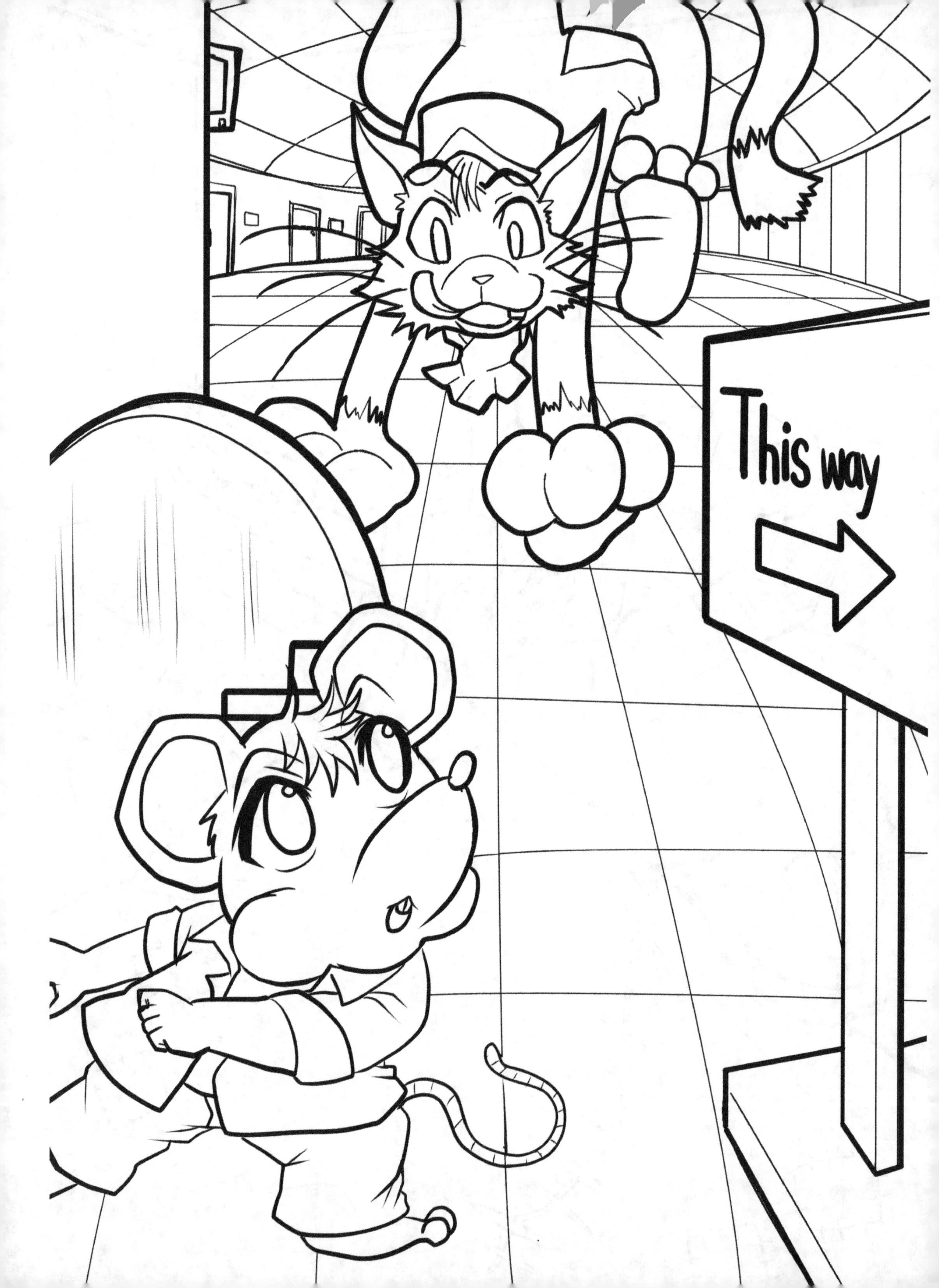
This way

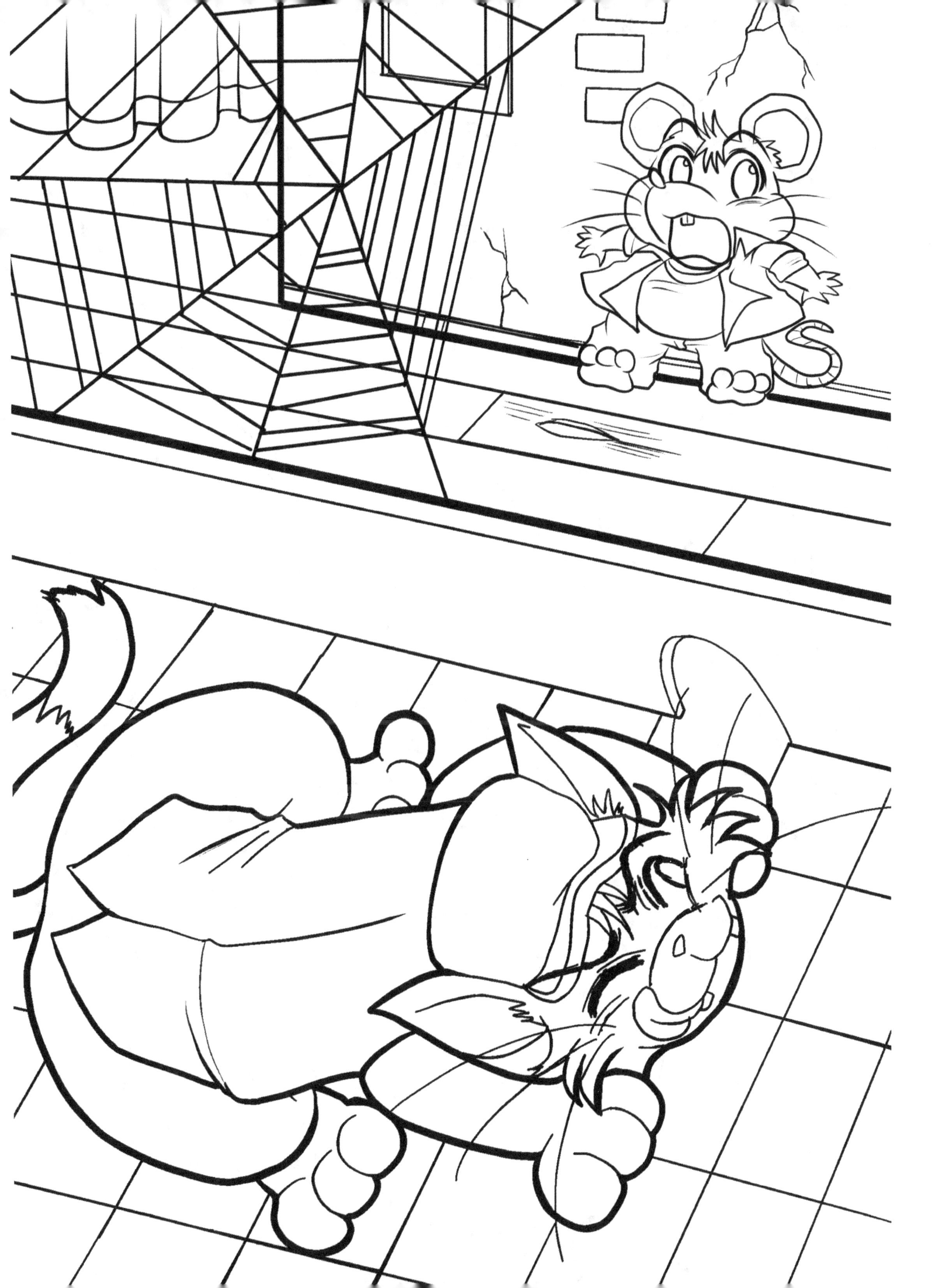

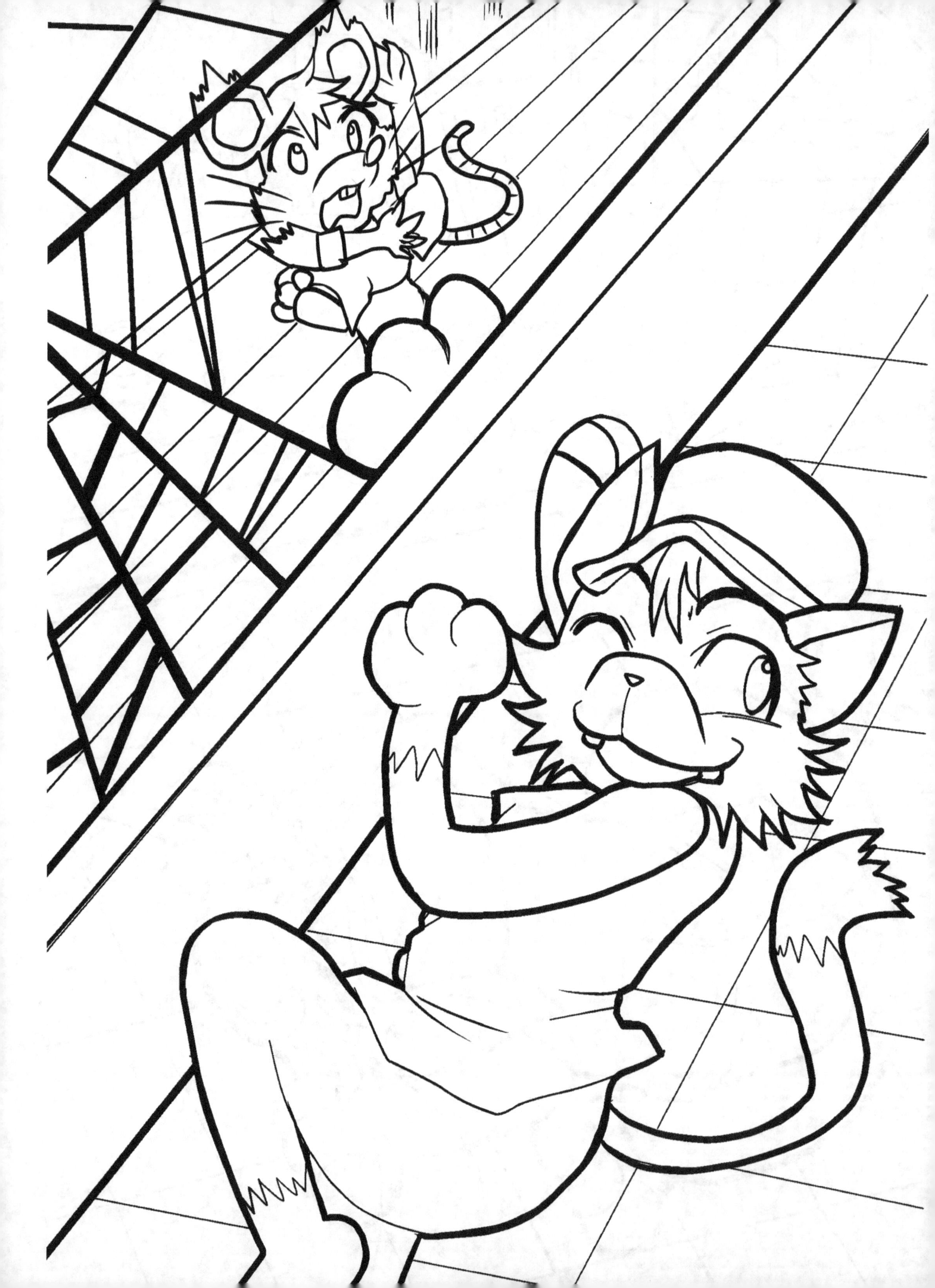

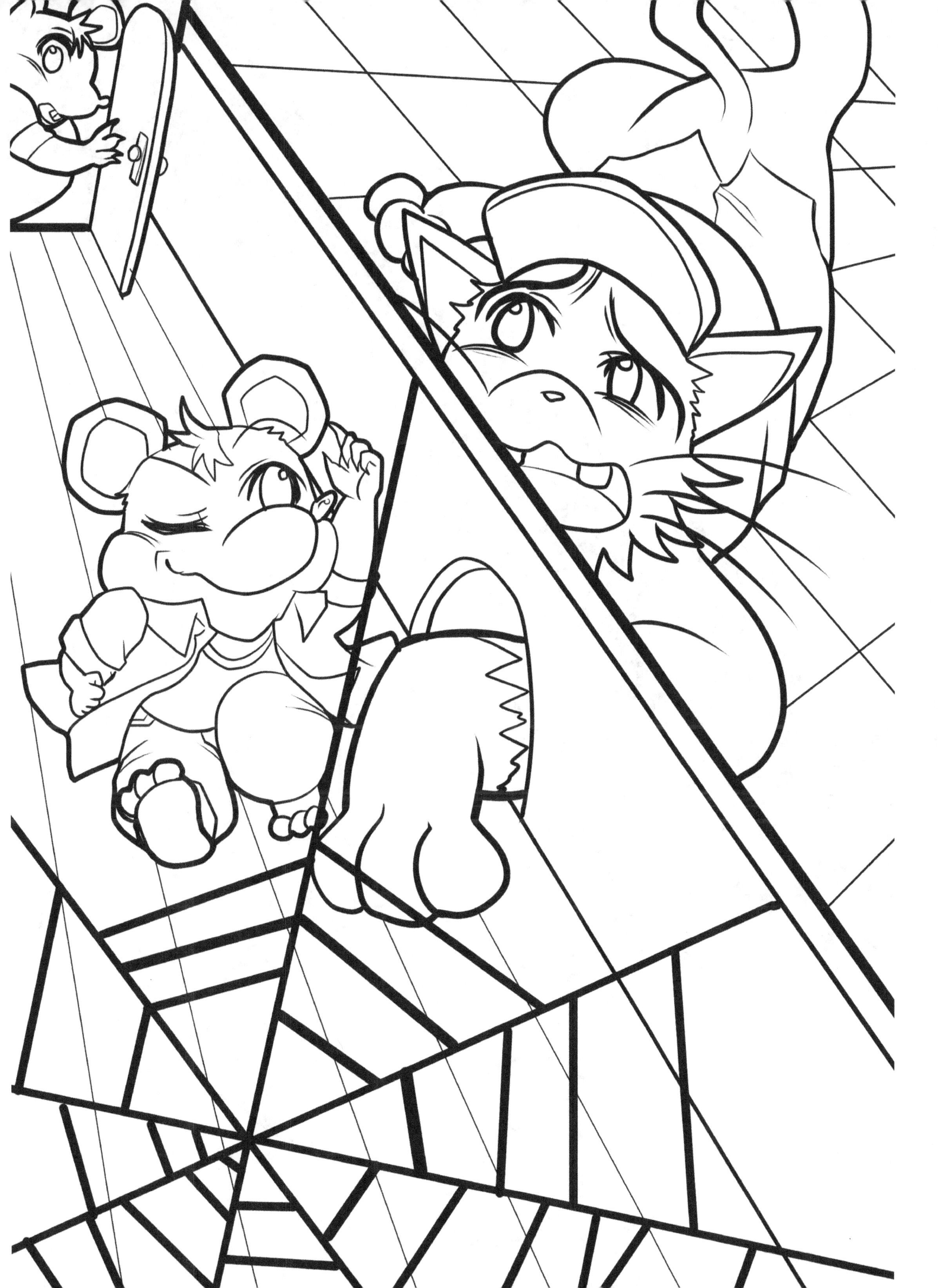

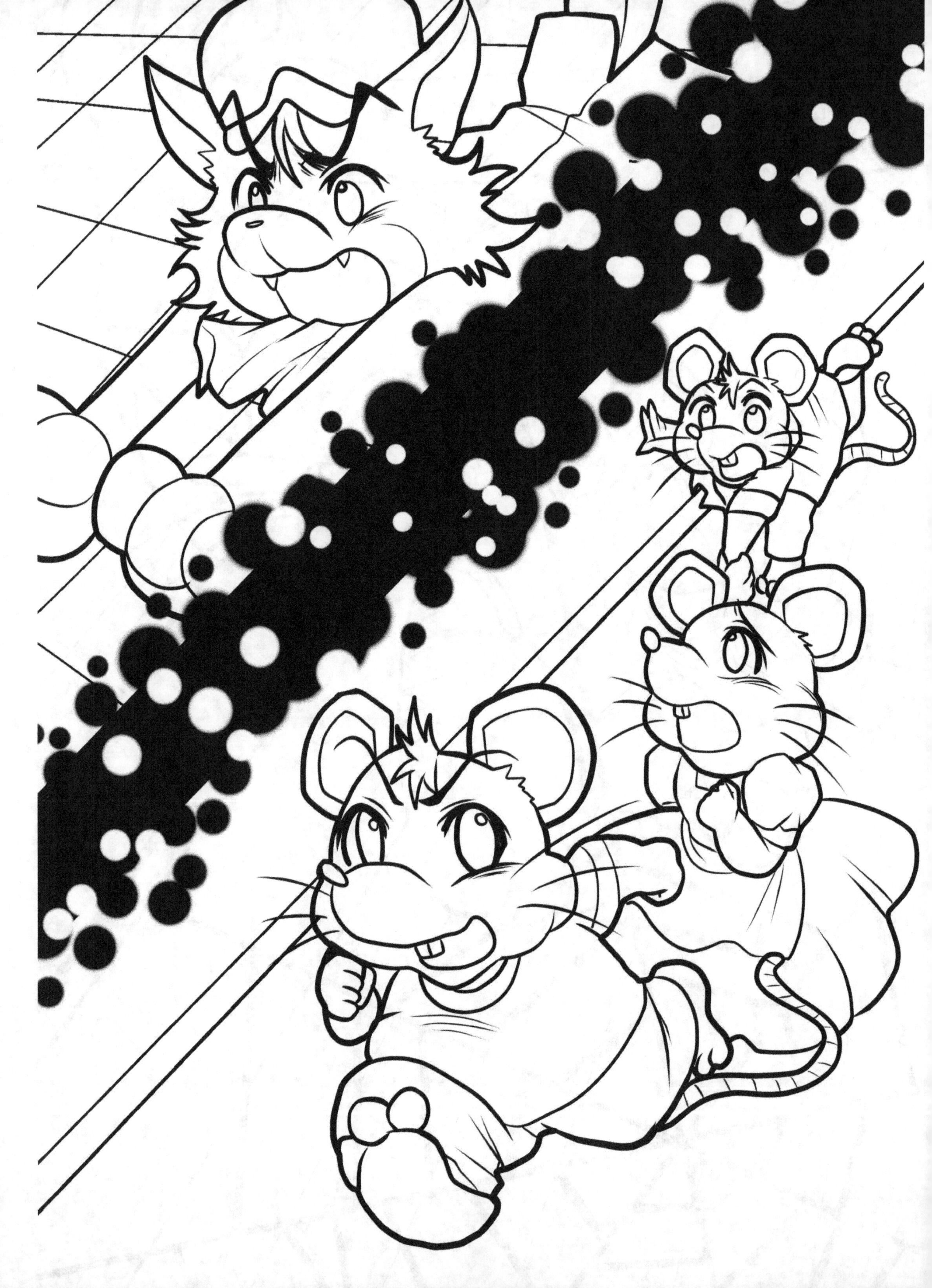

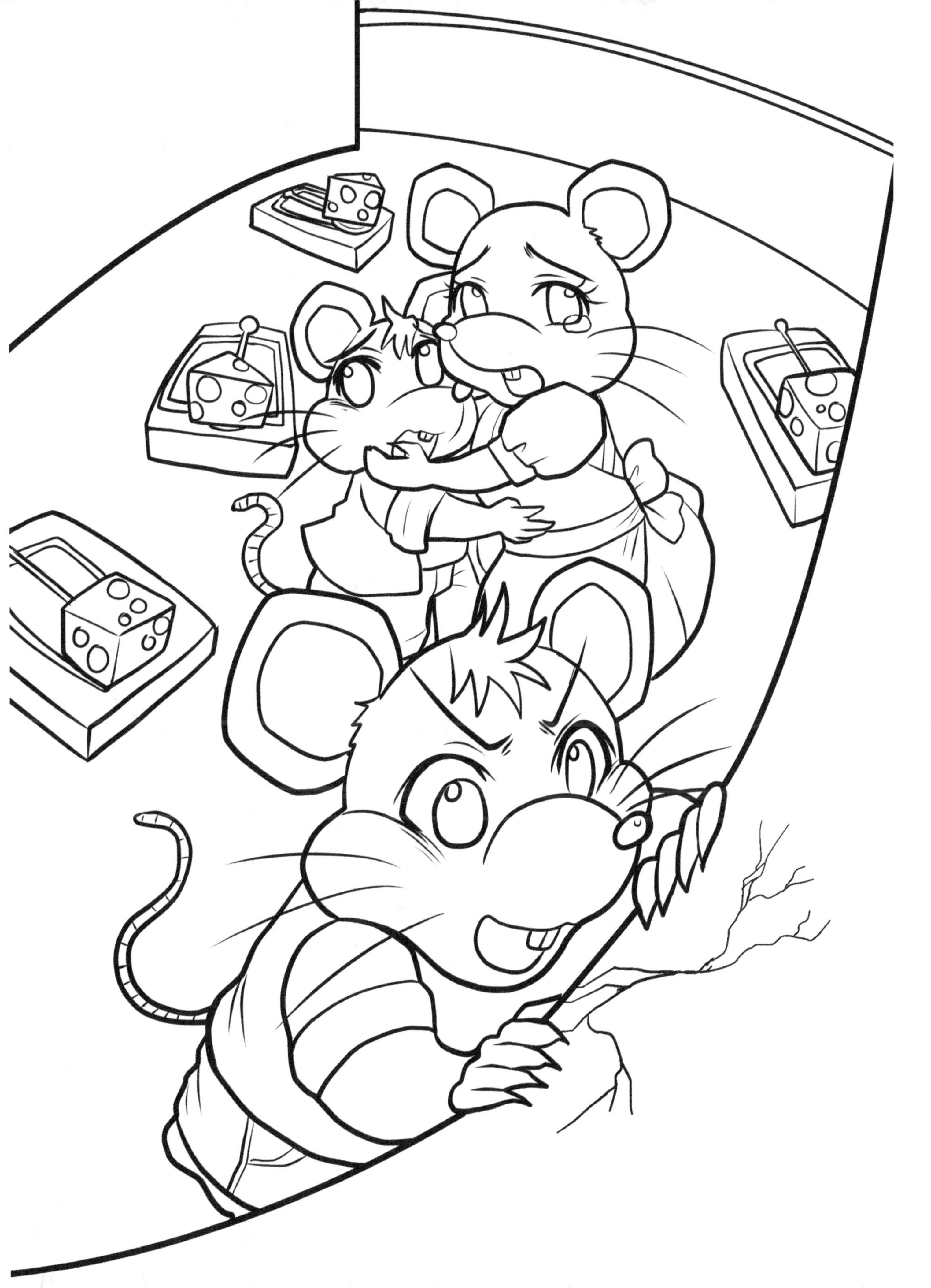

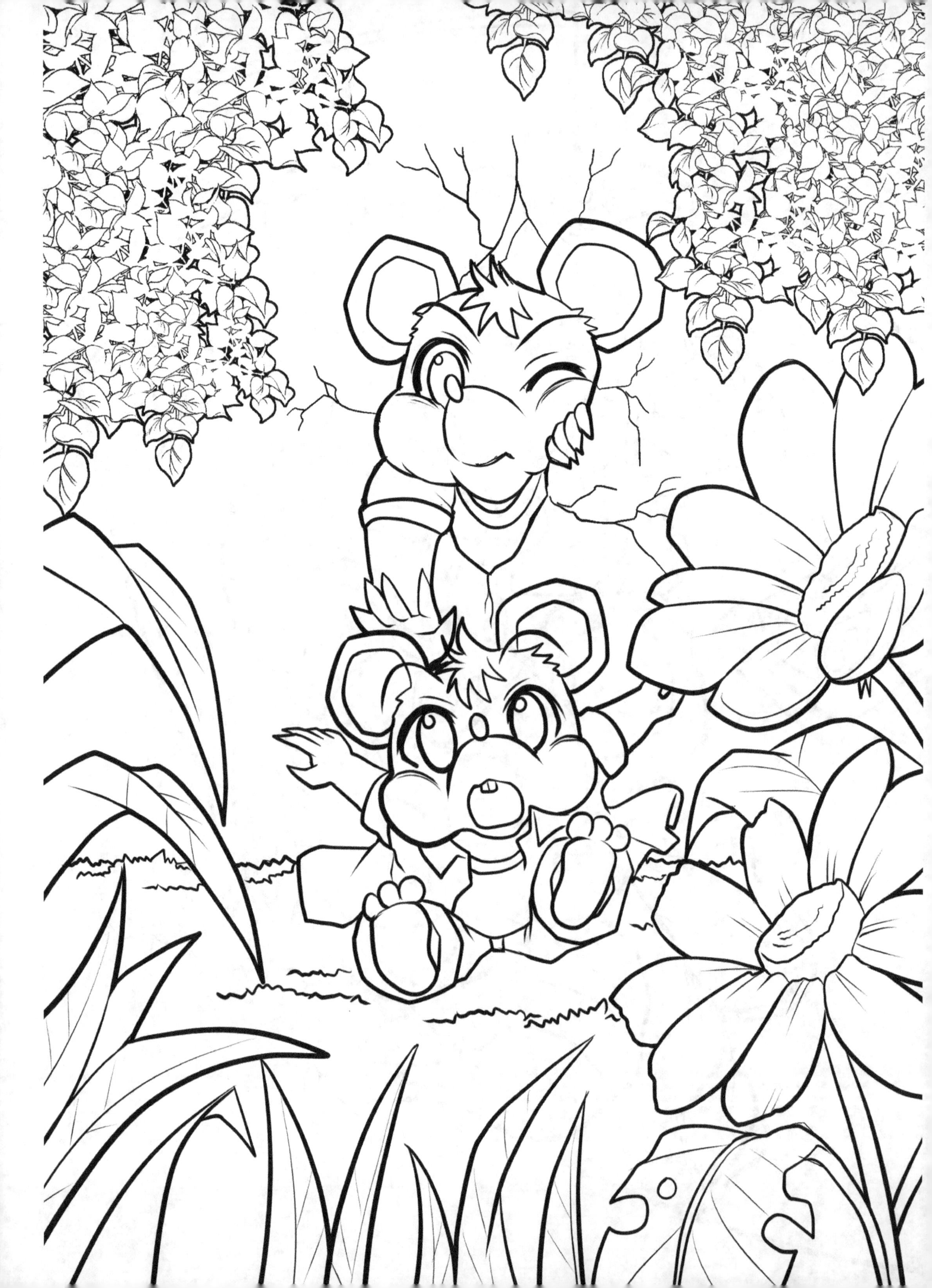

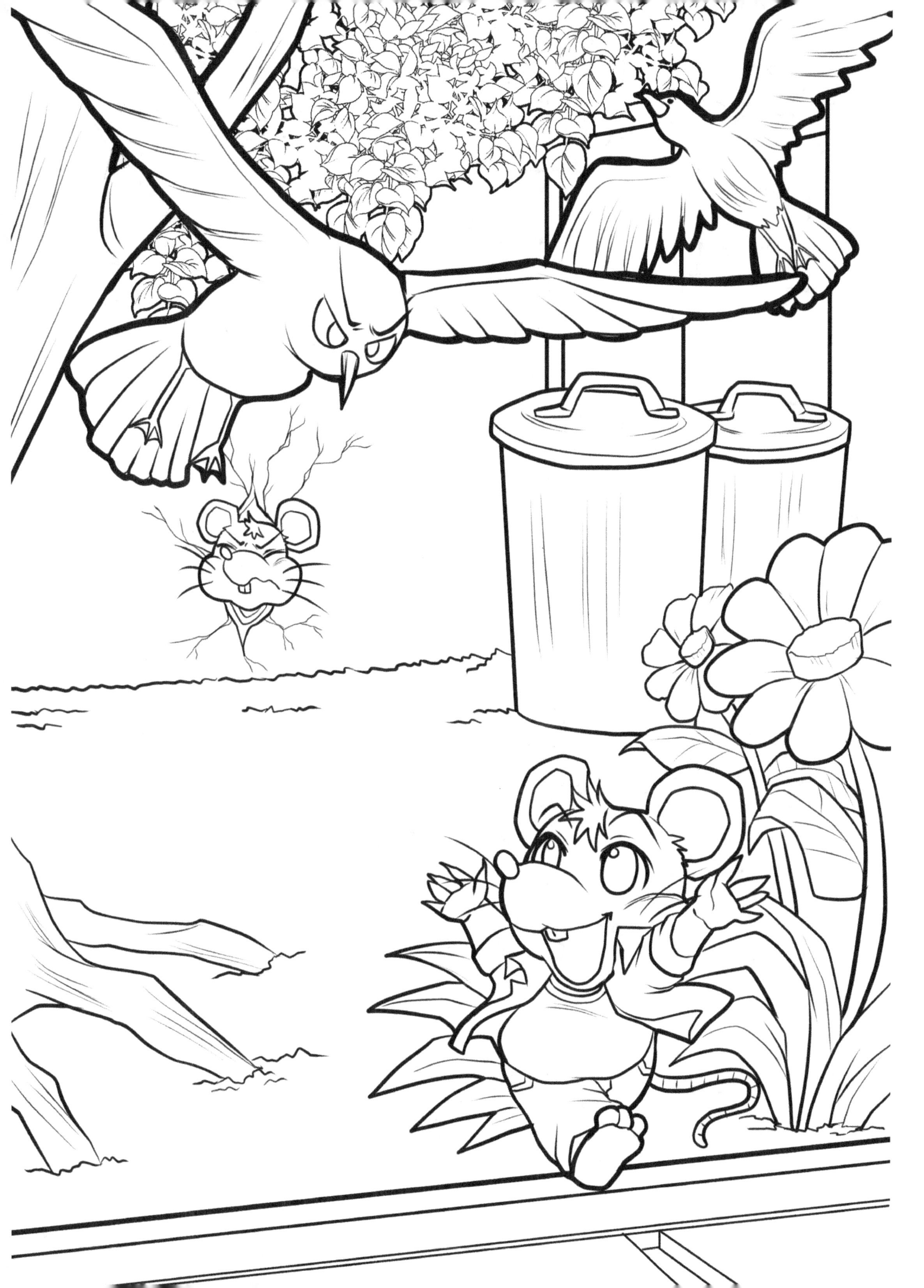

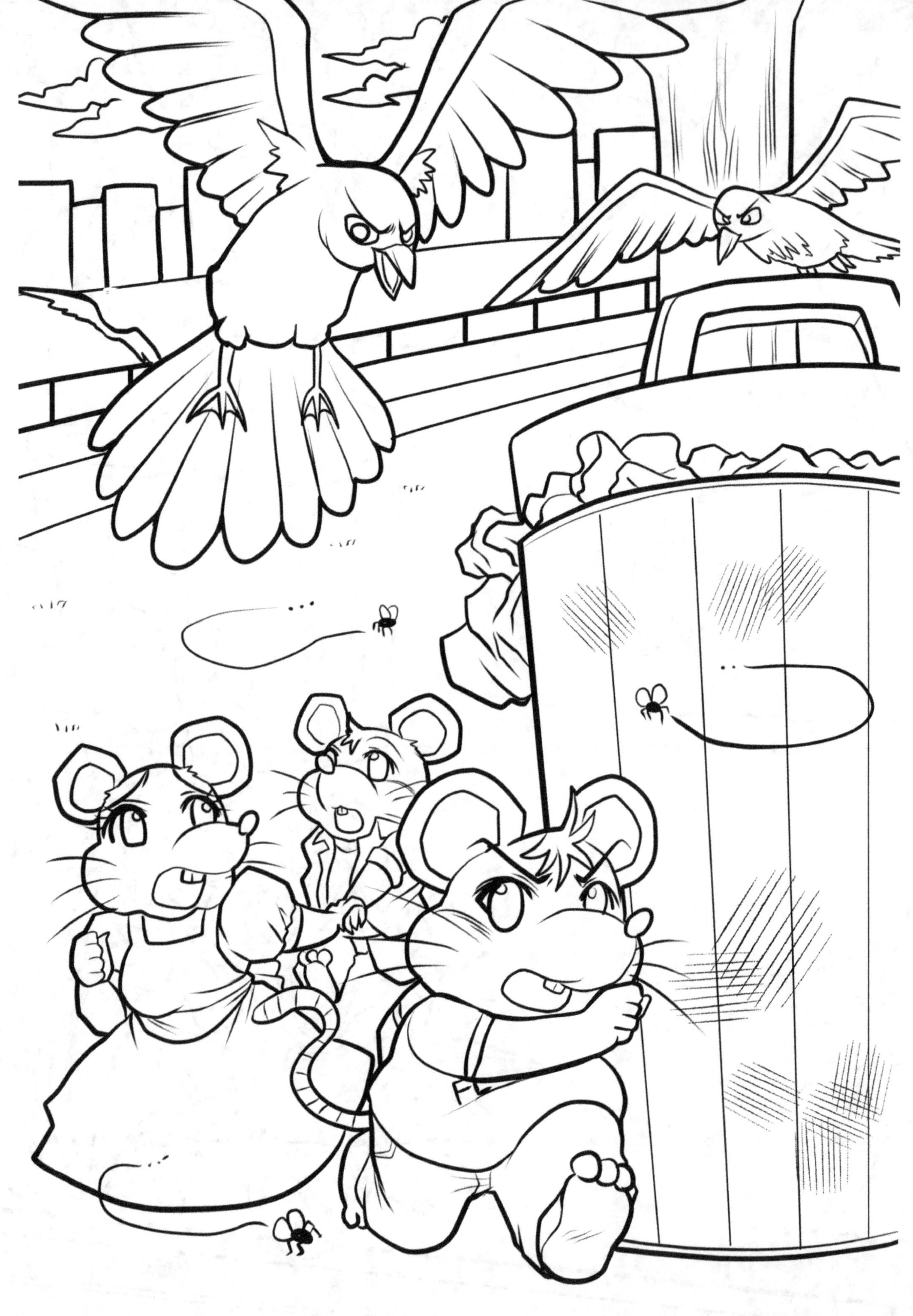

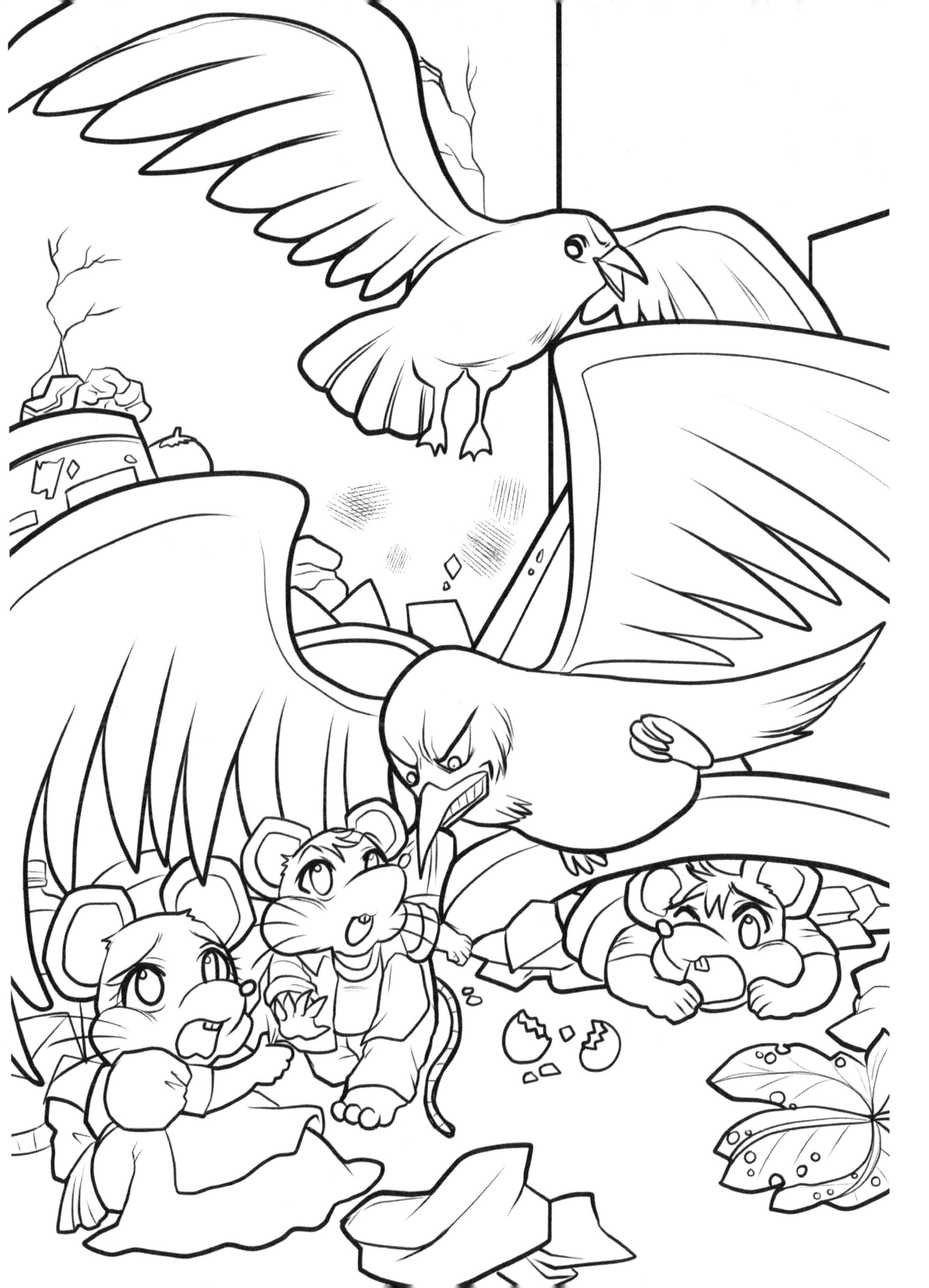

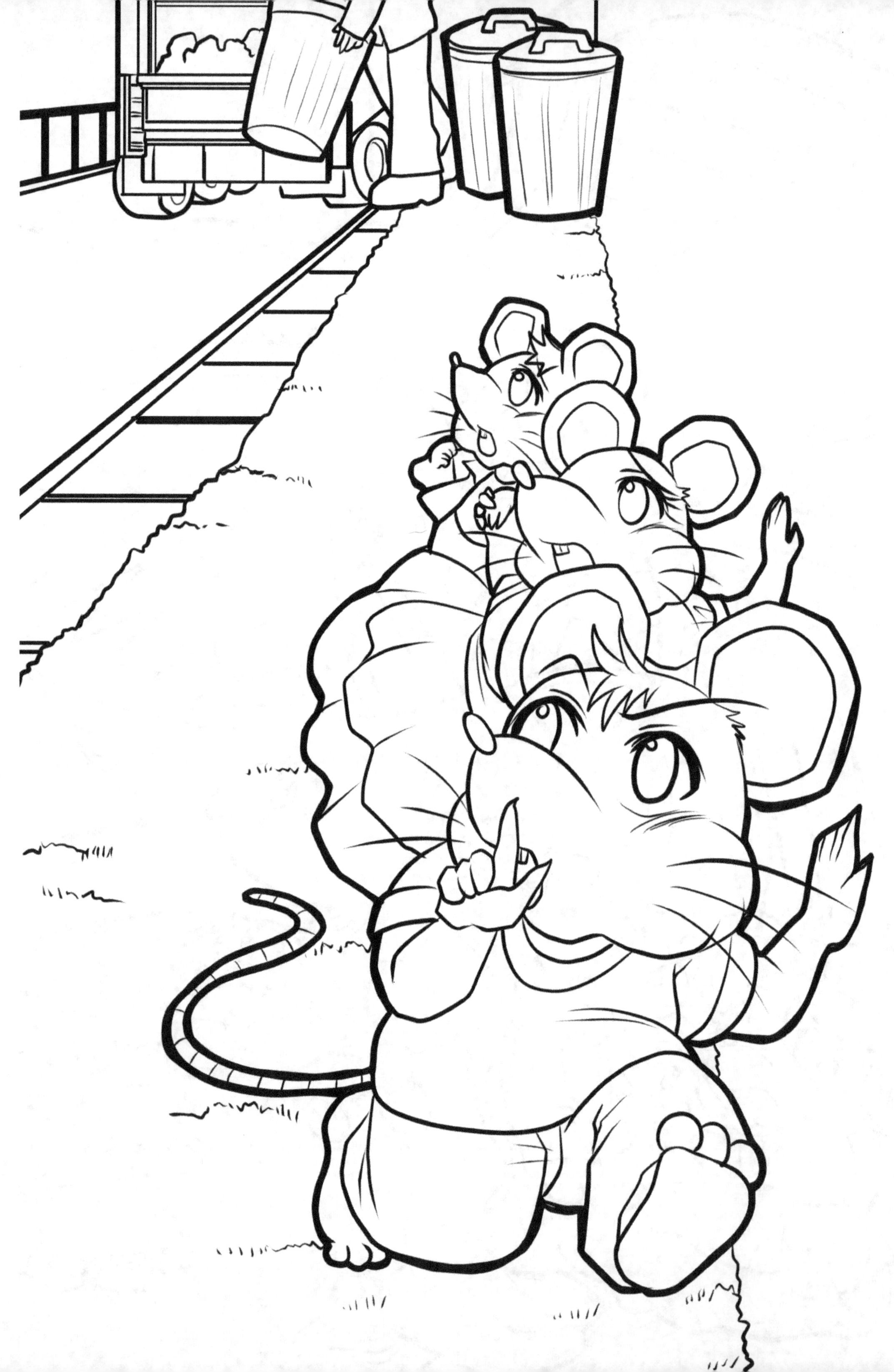

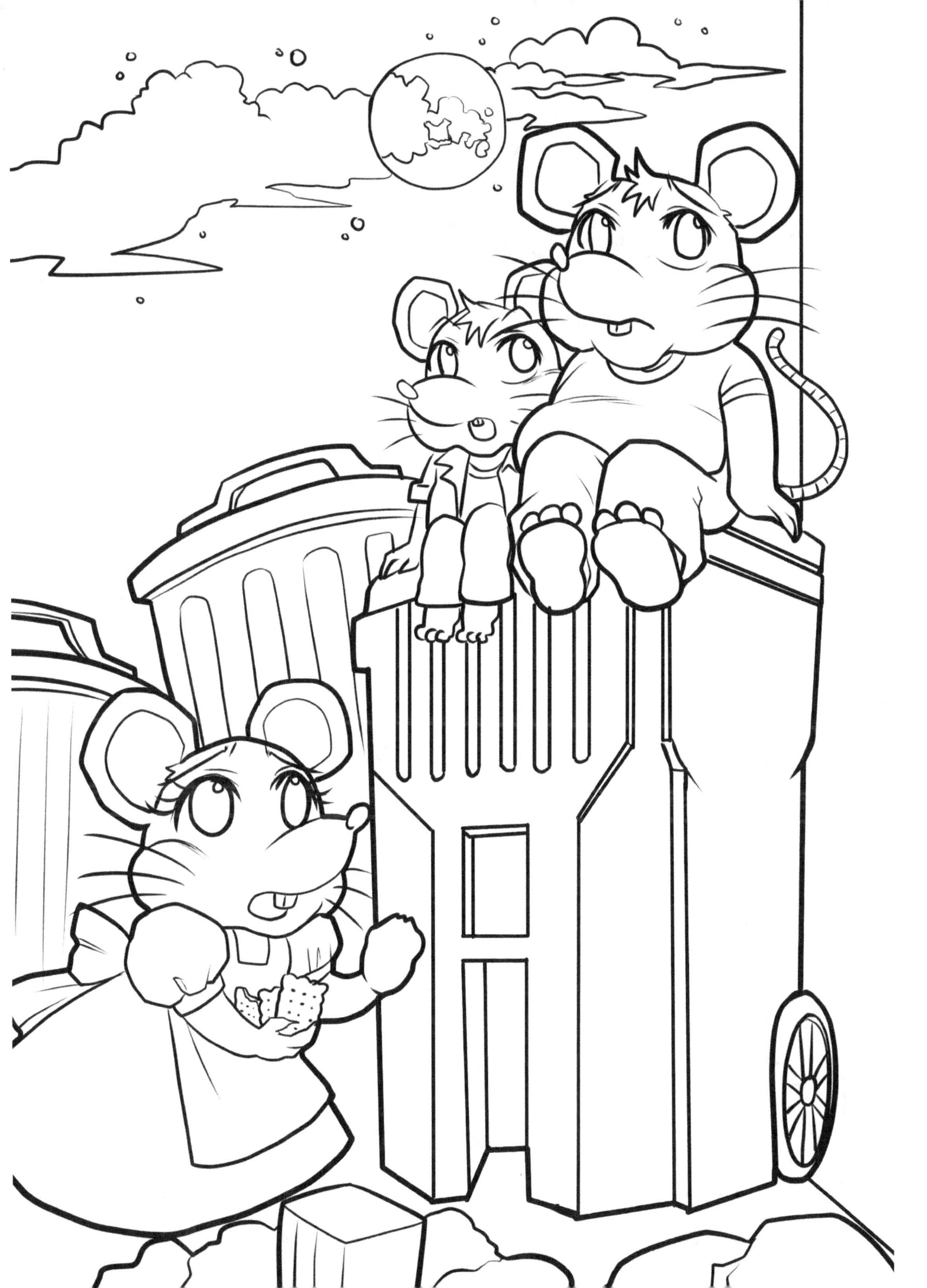

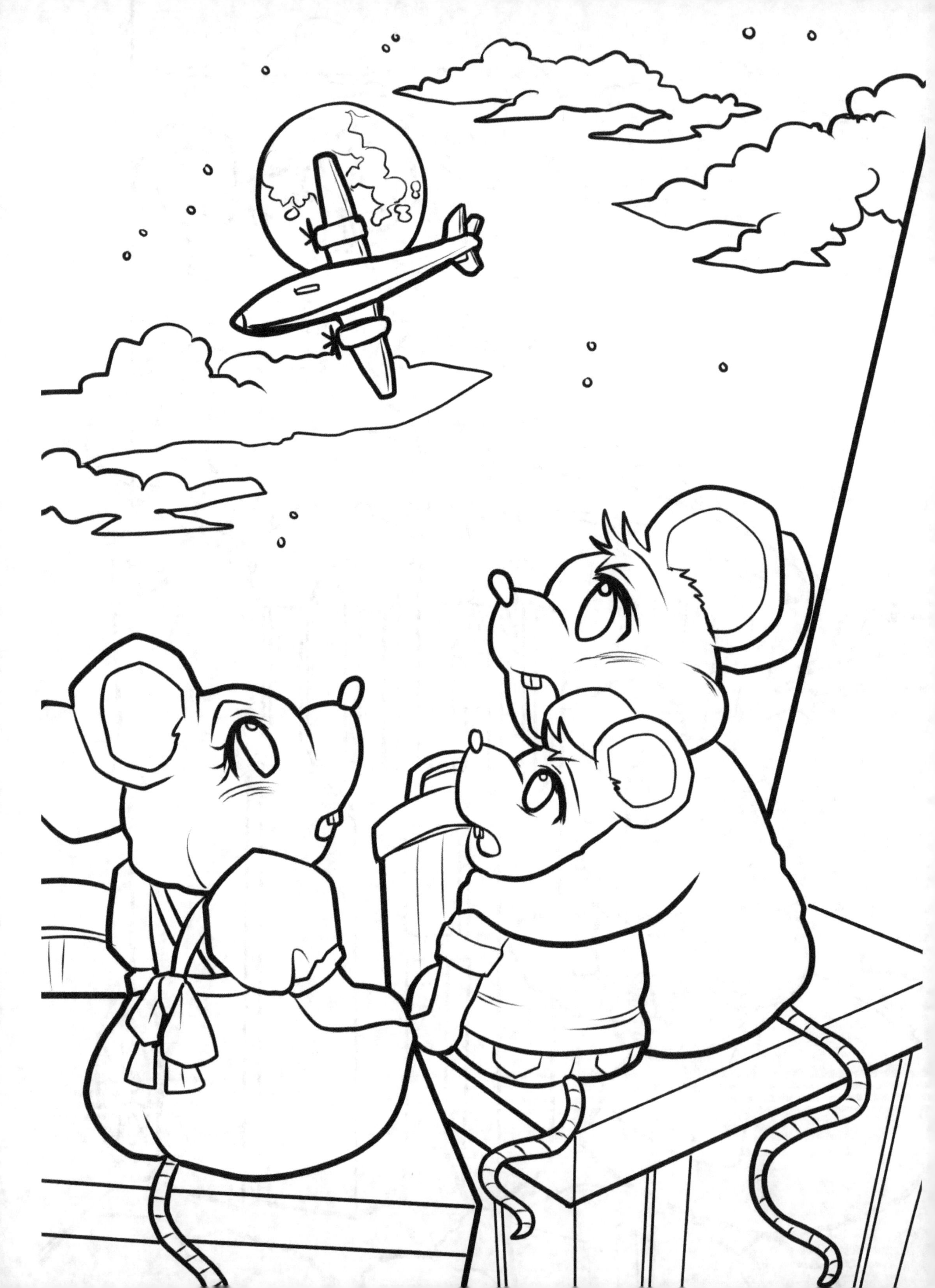

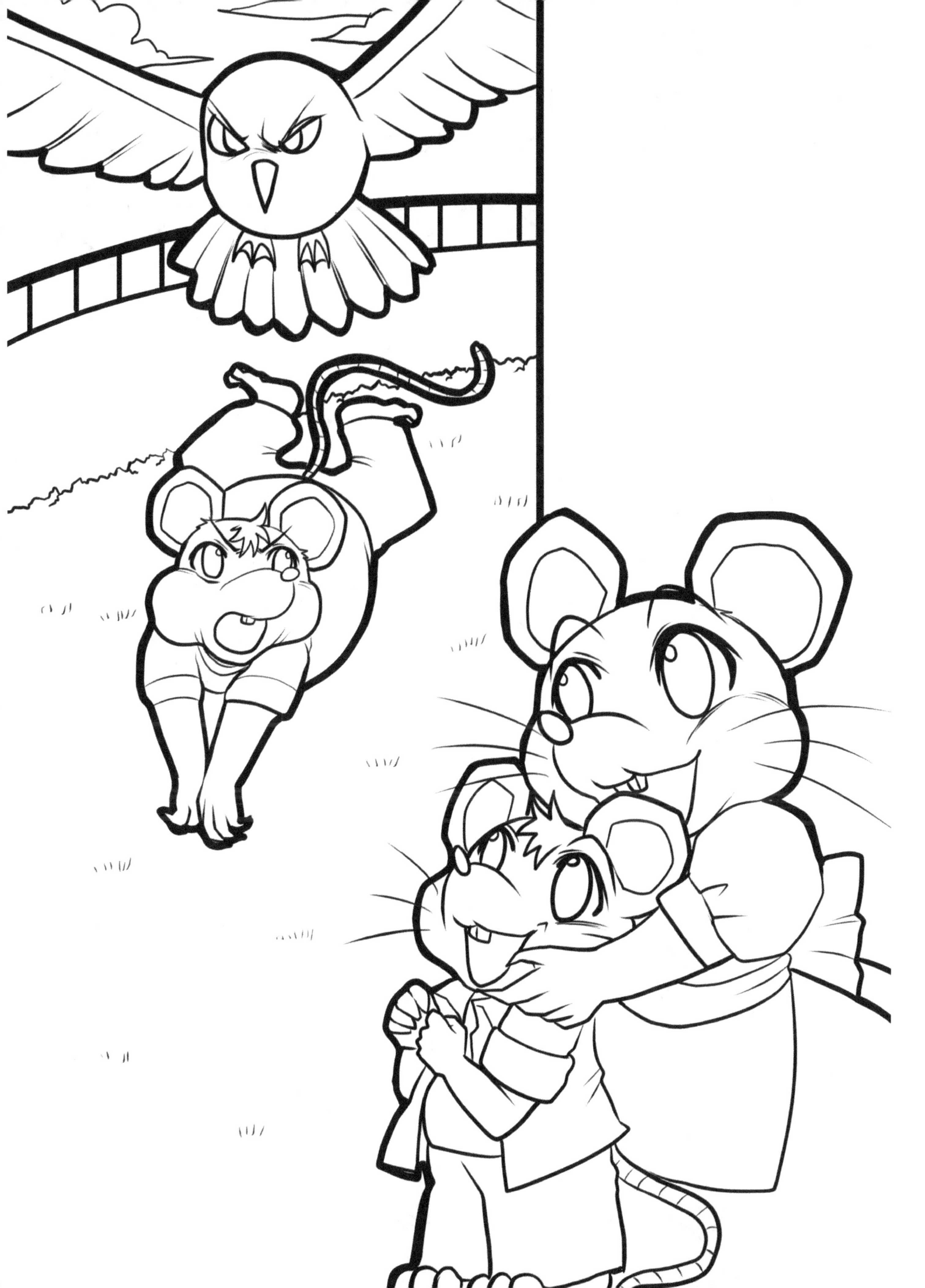

MOUSE MAZE

One mouse found the path
to the cheese. Can you find it too?

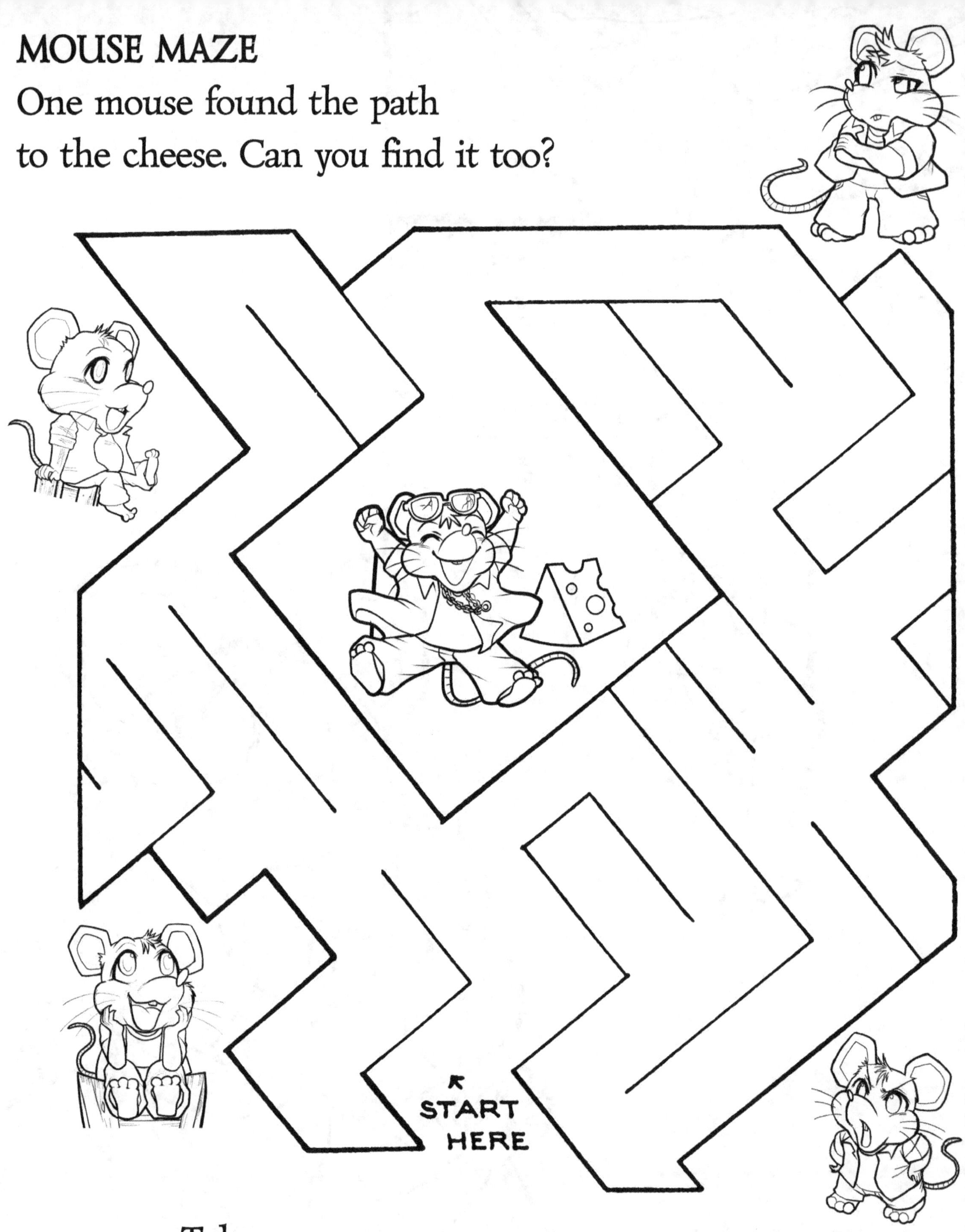

Take a crayon.
Draw between the lines. Do not cross over a line.
If the path stops, go back and try a new path.

Fill in the blanks!

can __________
and __________ but
can't __________ .

can __________
and __________ but
can't __________ .

can __________
and __________ but
can't __________ .

can __________
and __________ but
can't __________ .

can __________
and __________ but
can't __________ .

can __________
and __________ but
can't __________ .

can __________
and __________ but
can't __________ .

can __________
and __________ but
can't __________ .

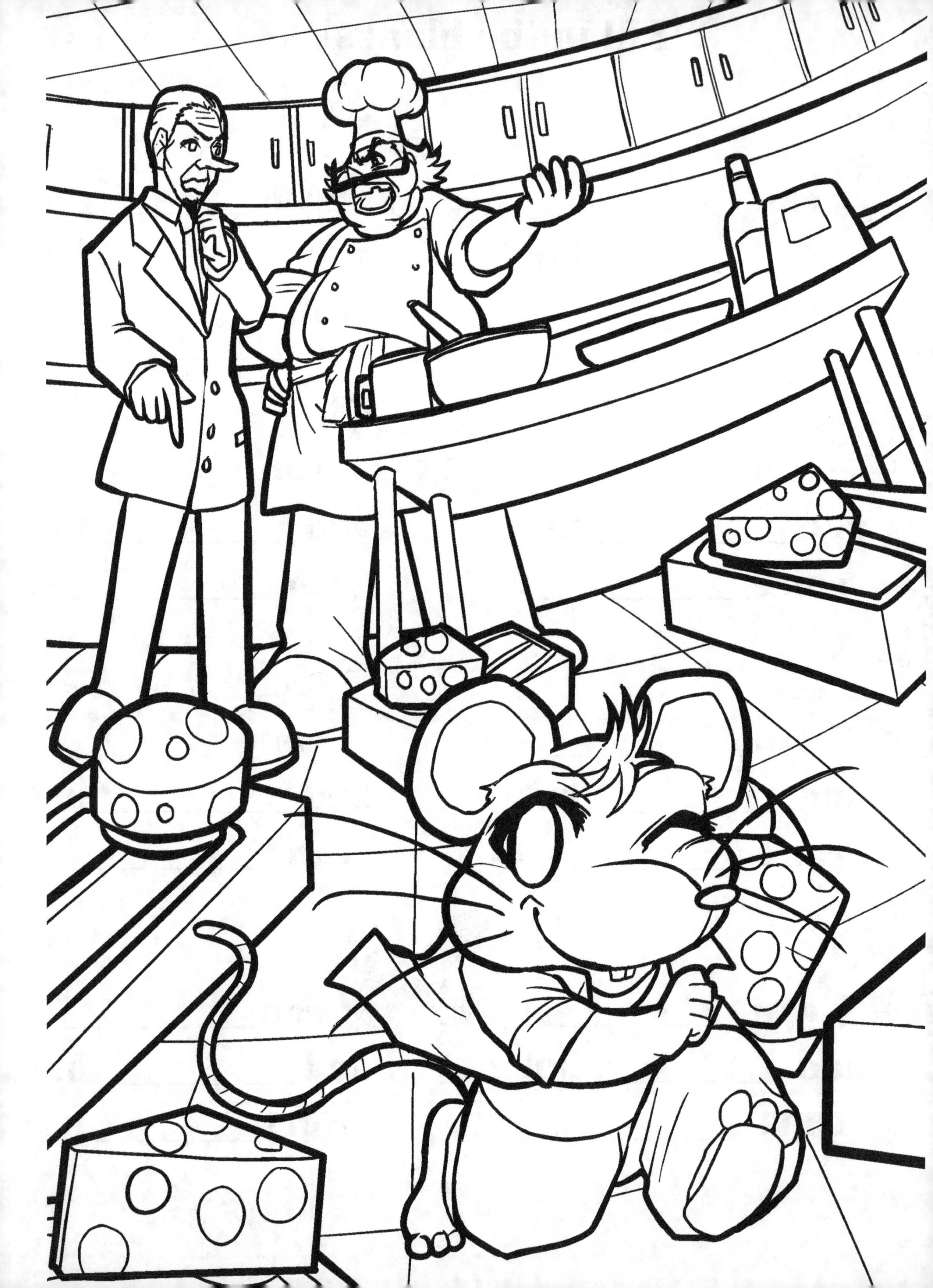

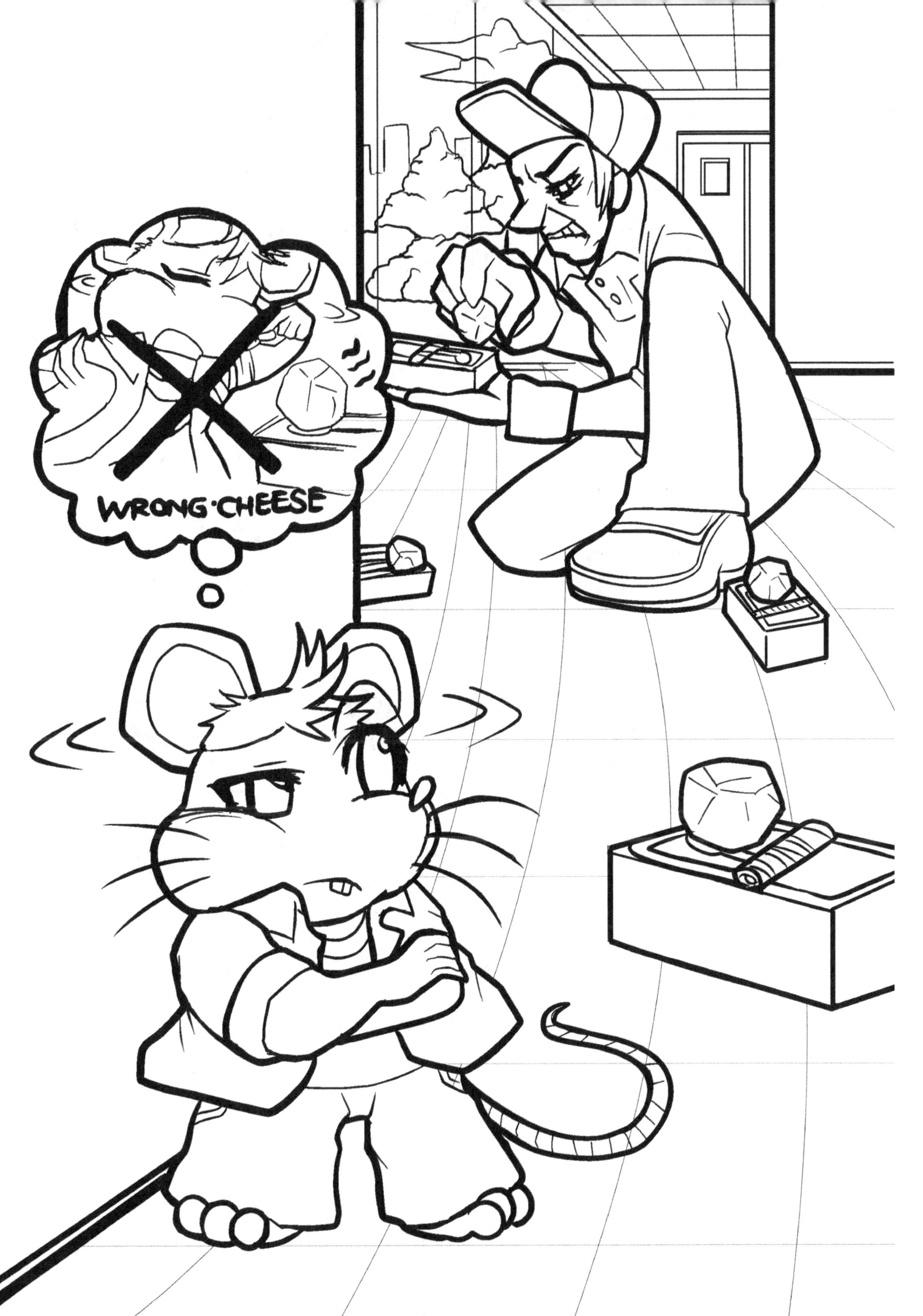

WRONG·CHEESE

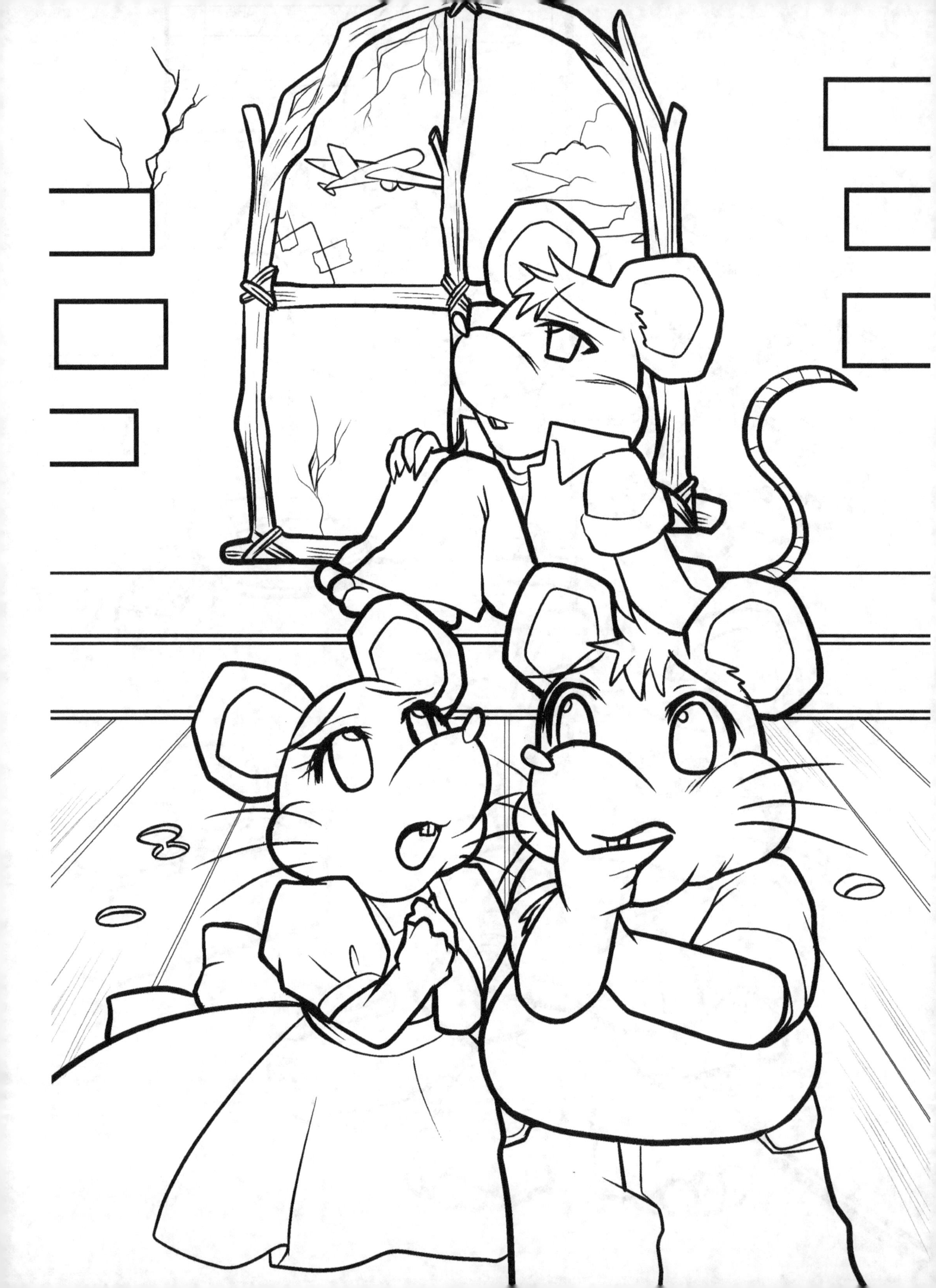

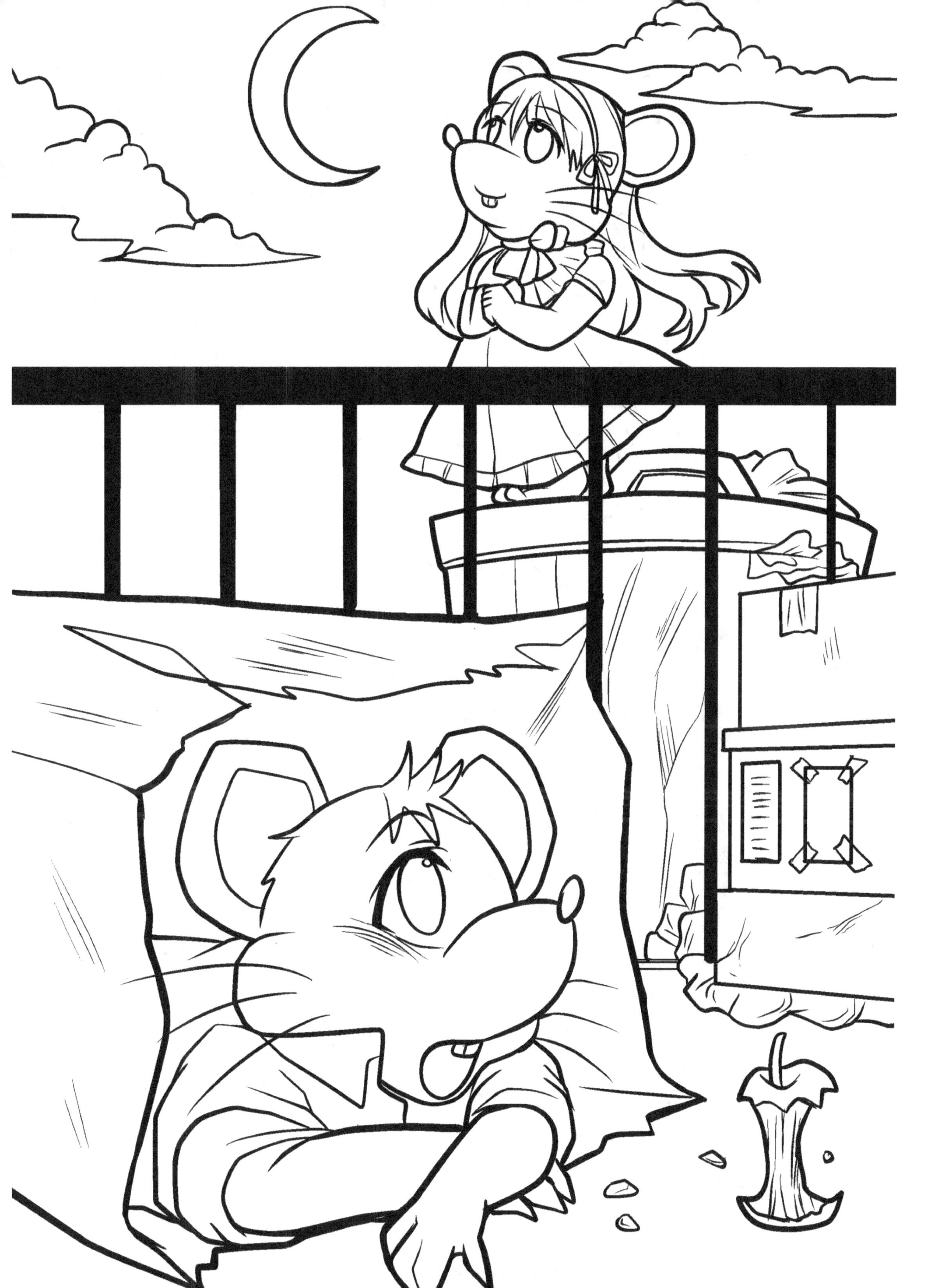

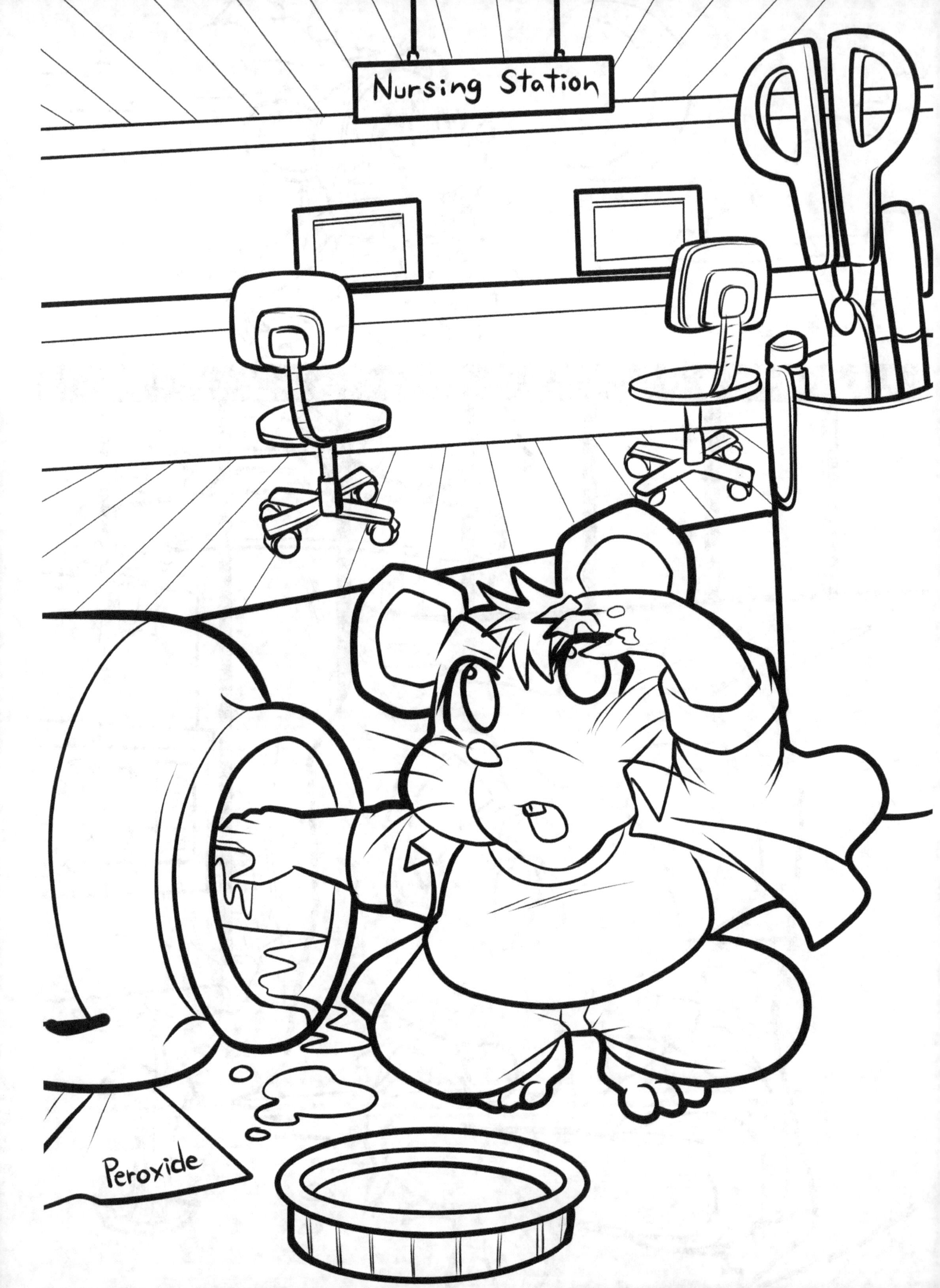
Nursing Station
Peroxide

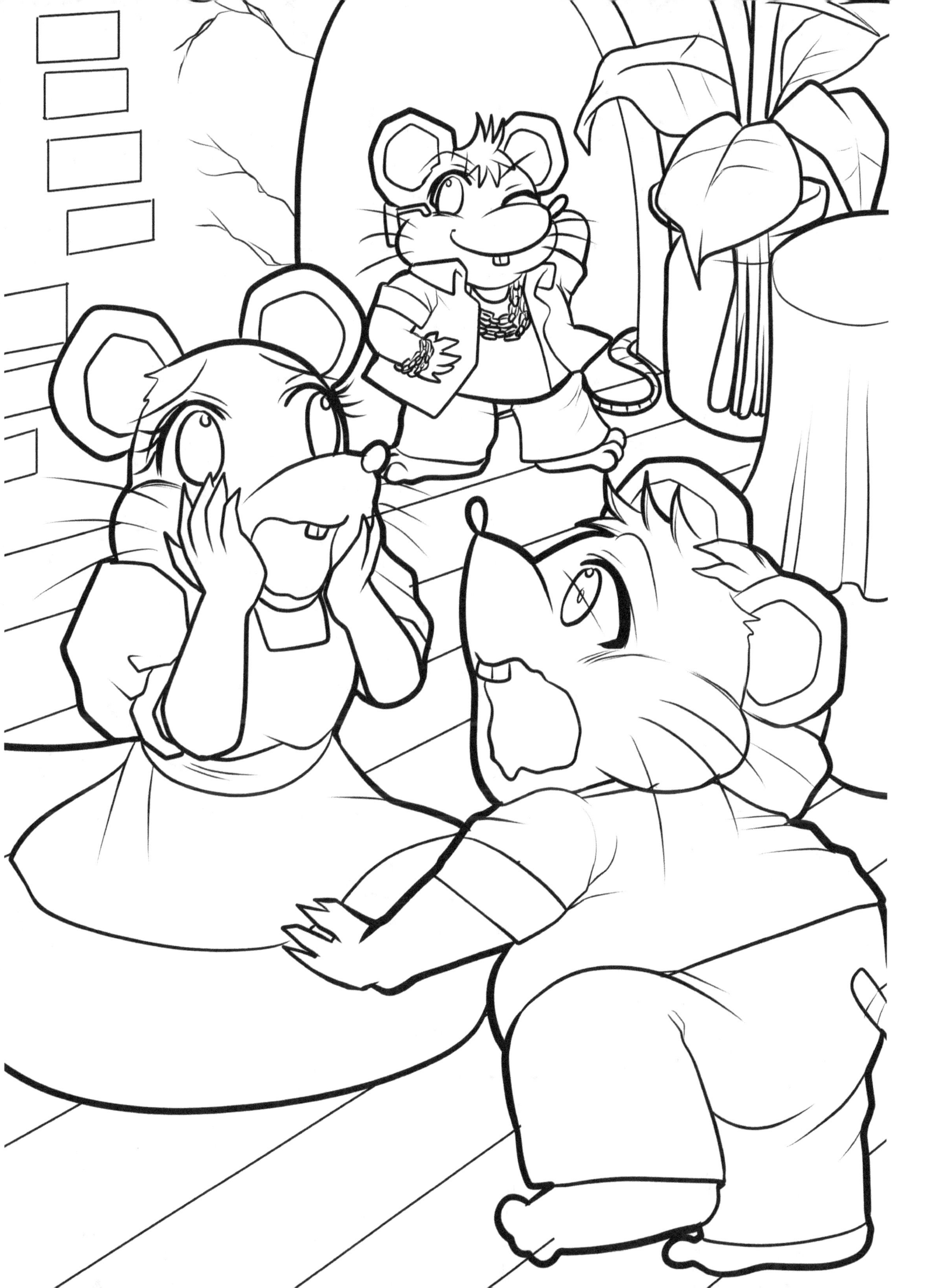

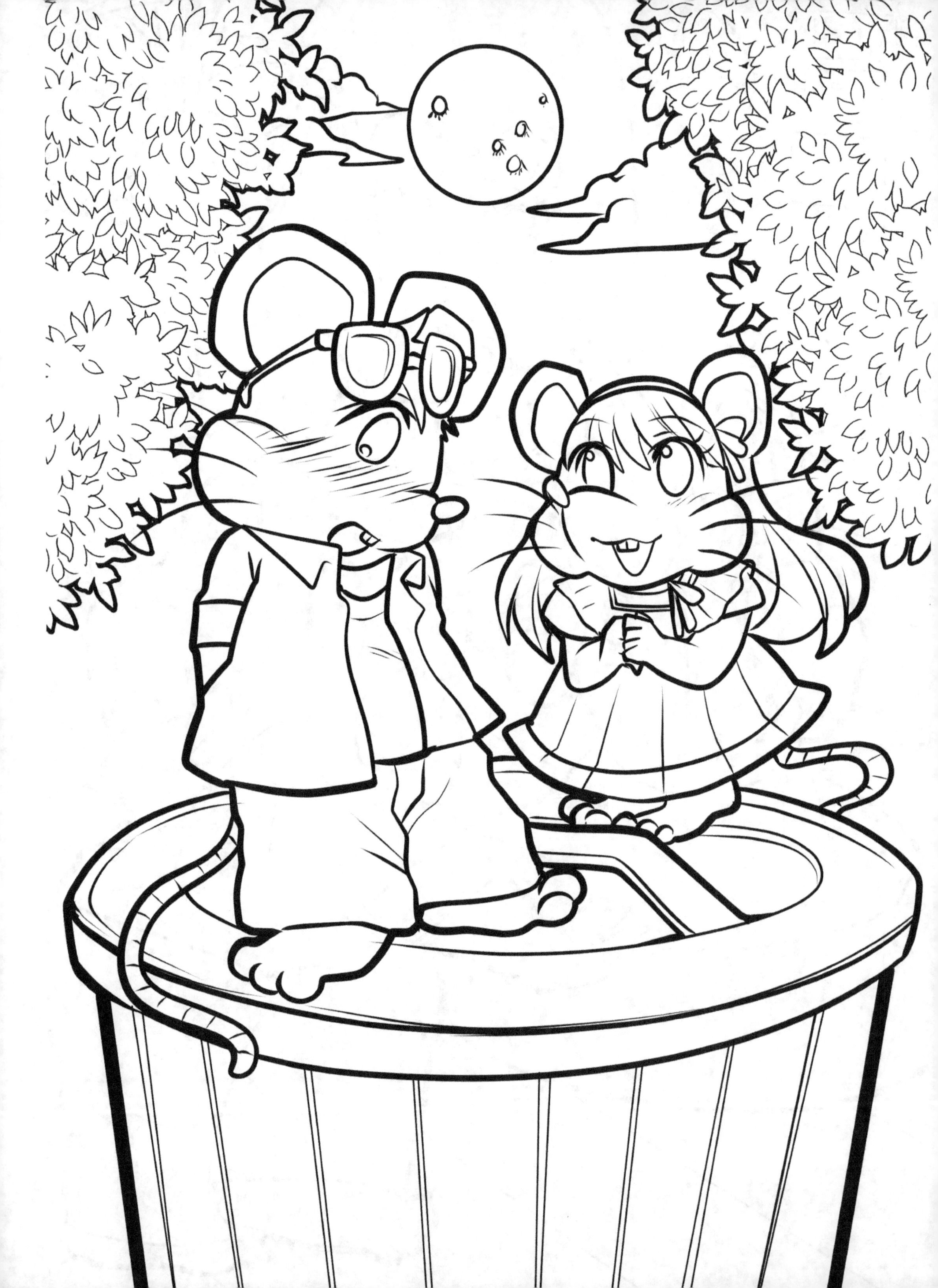

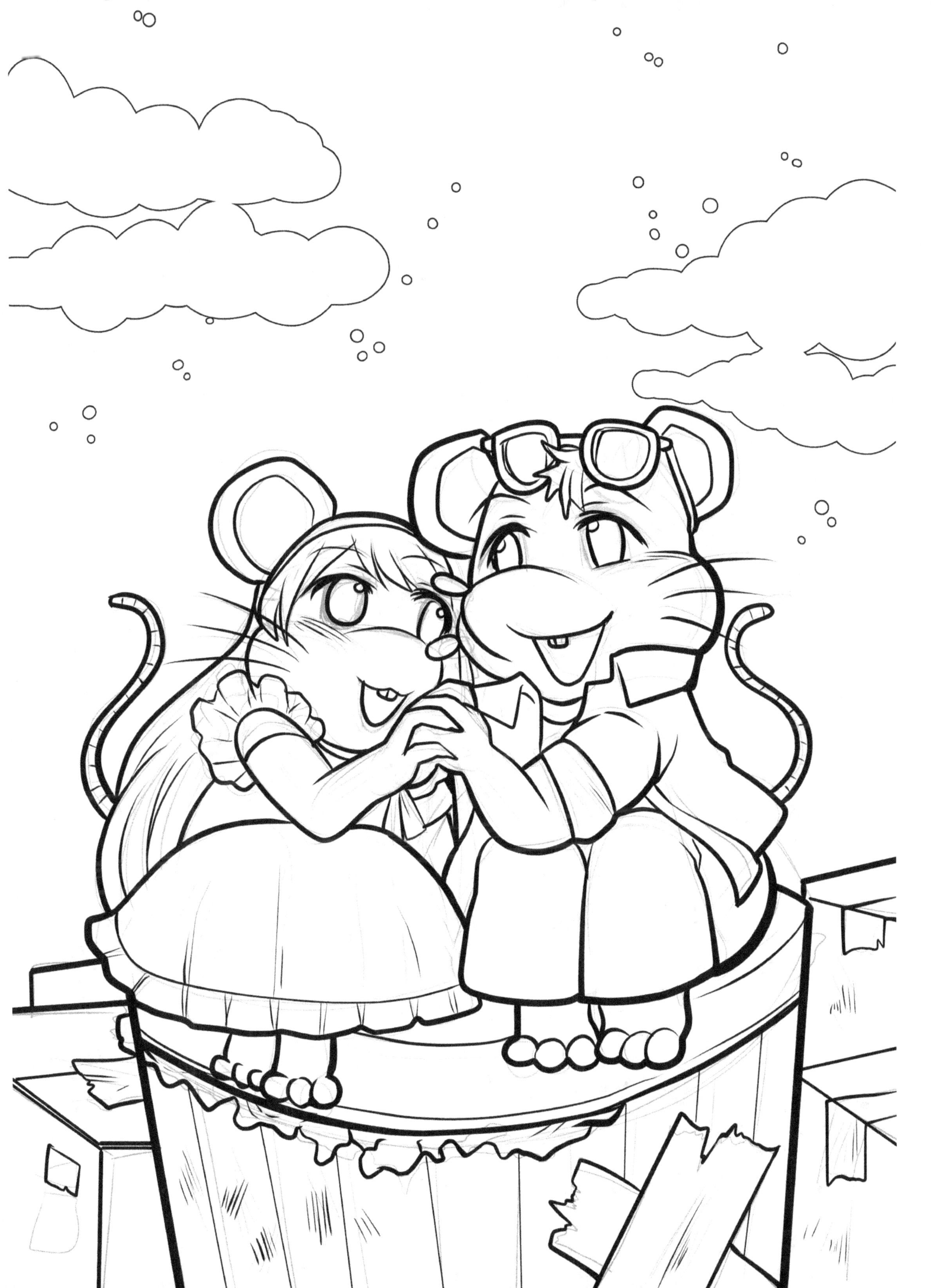

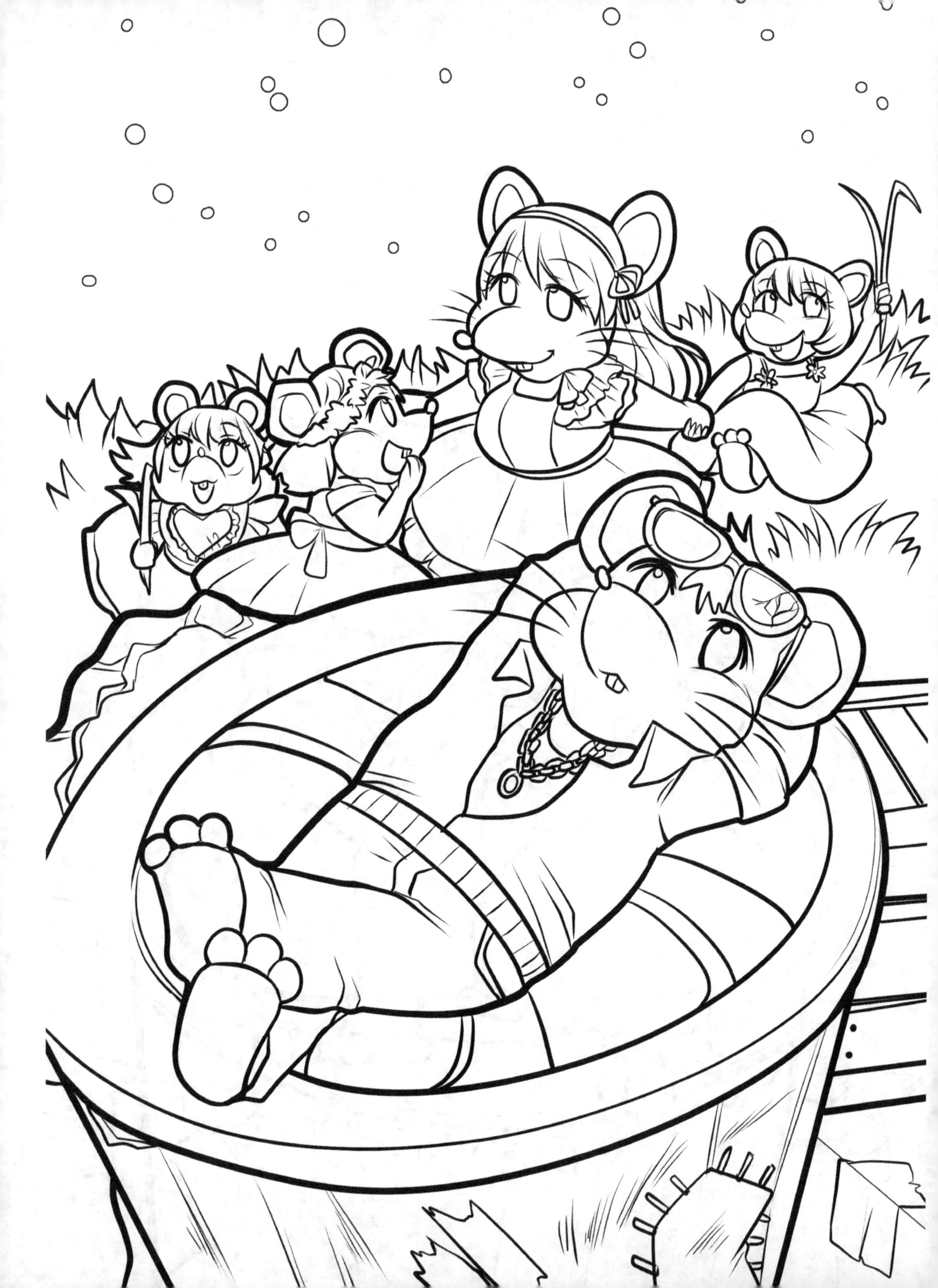

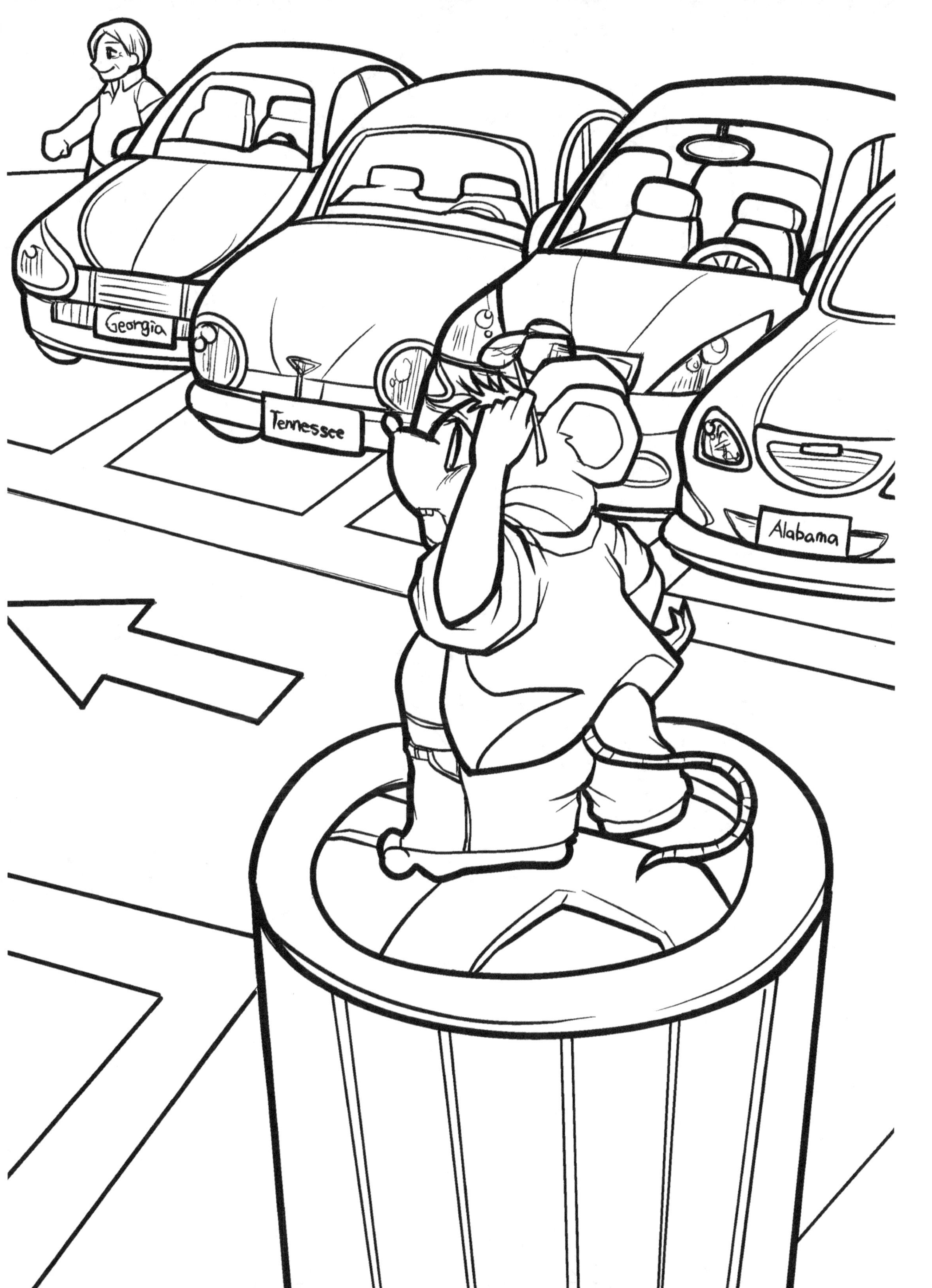

Georgia
Tennessee
Alabama

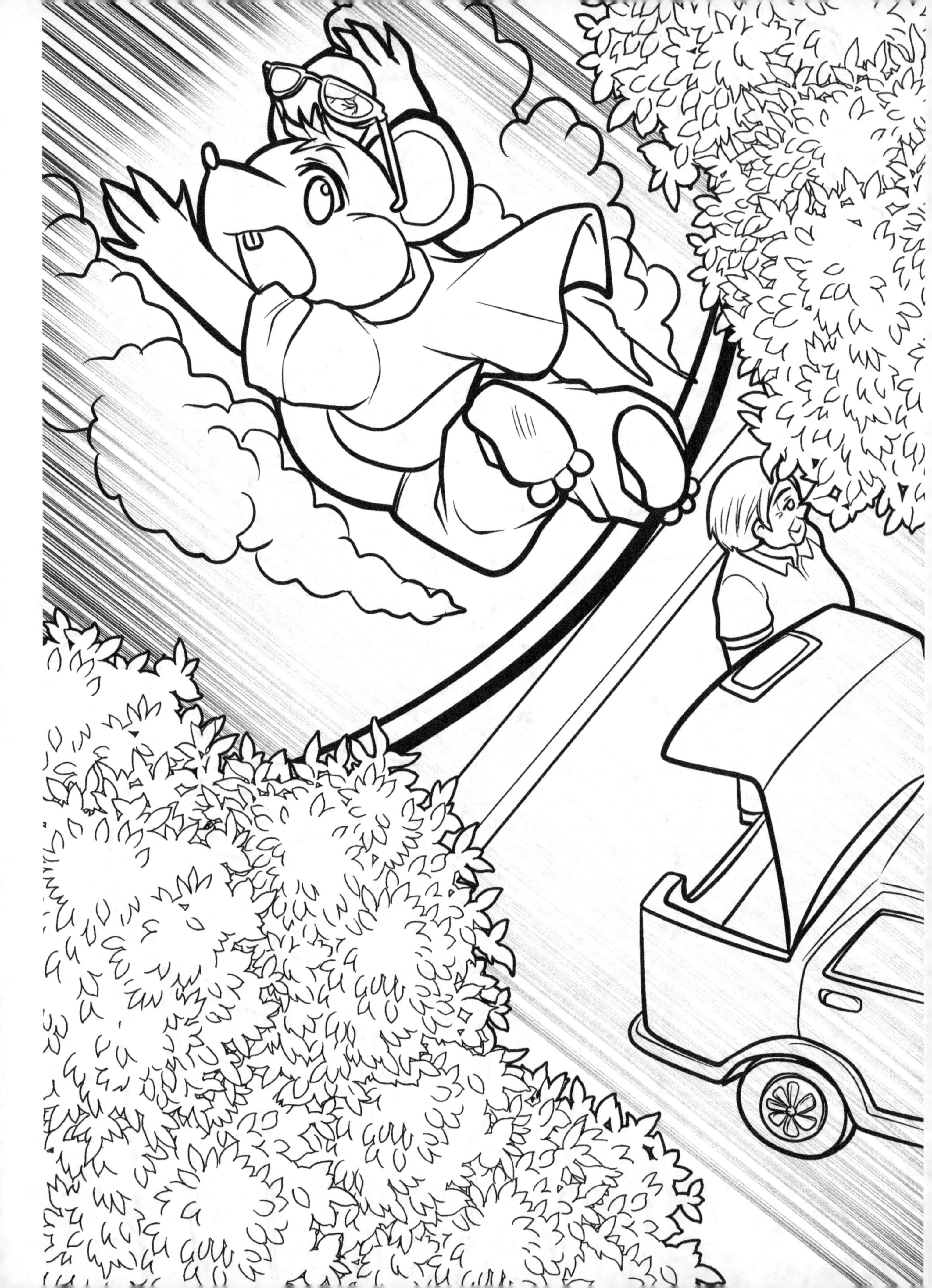

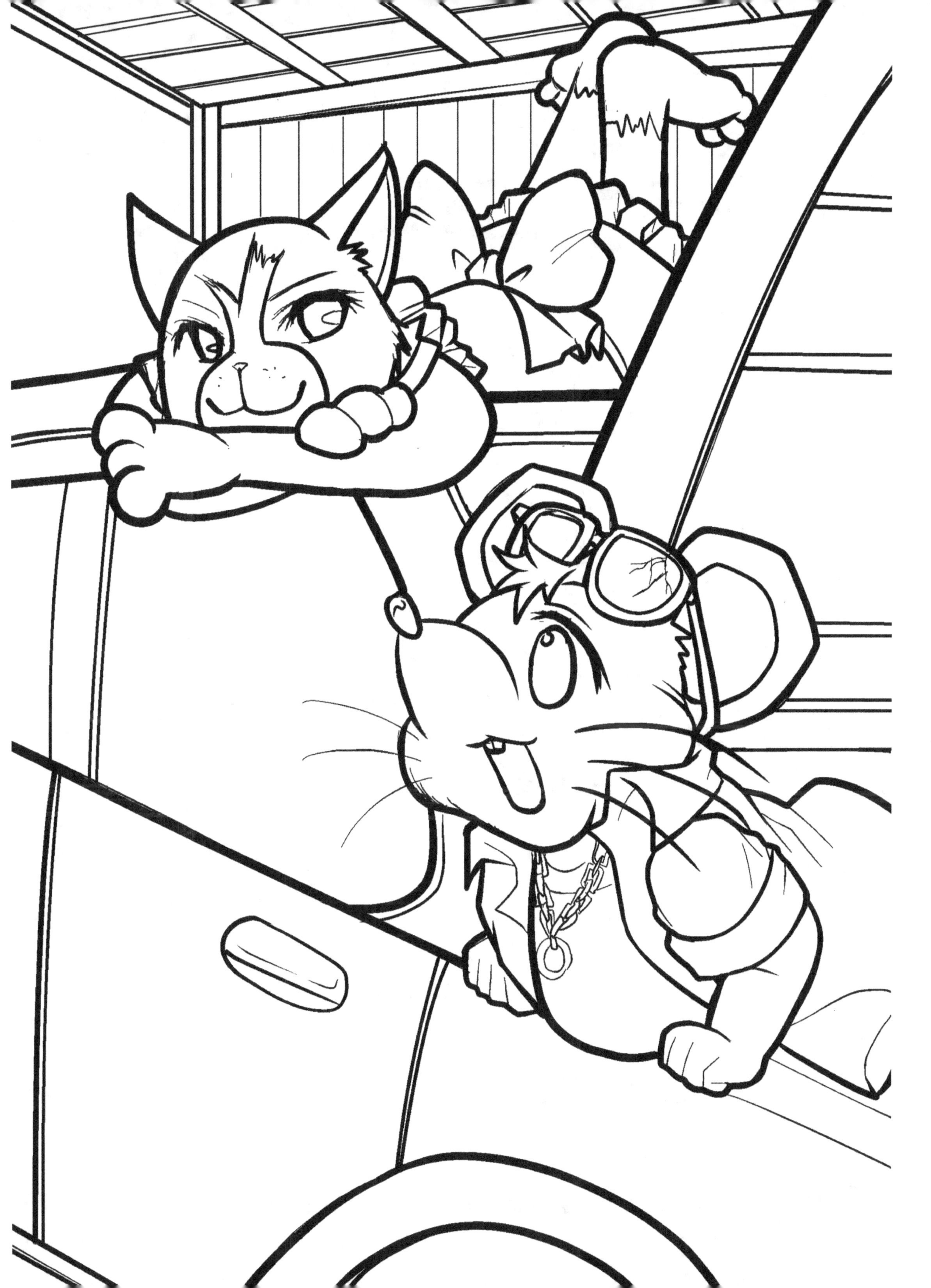

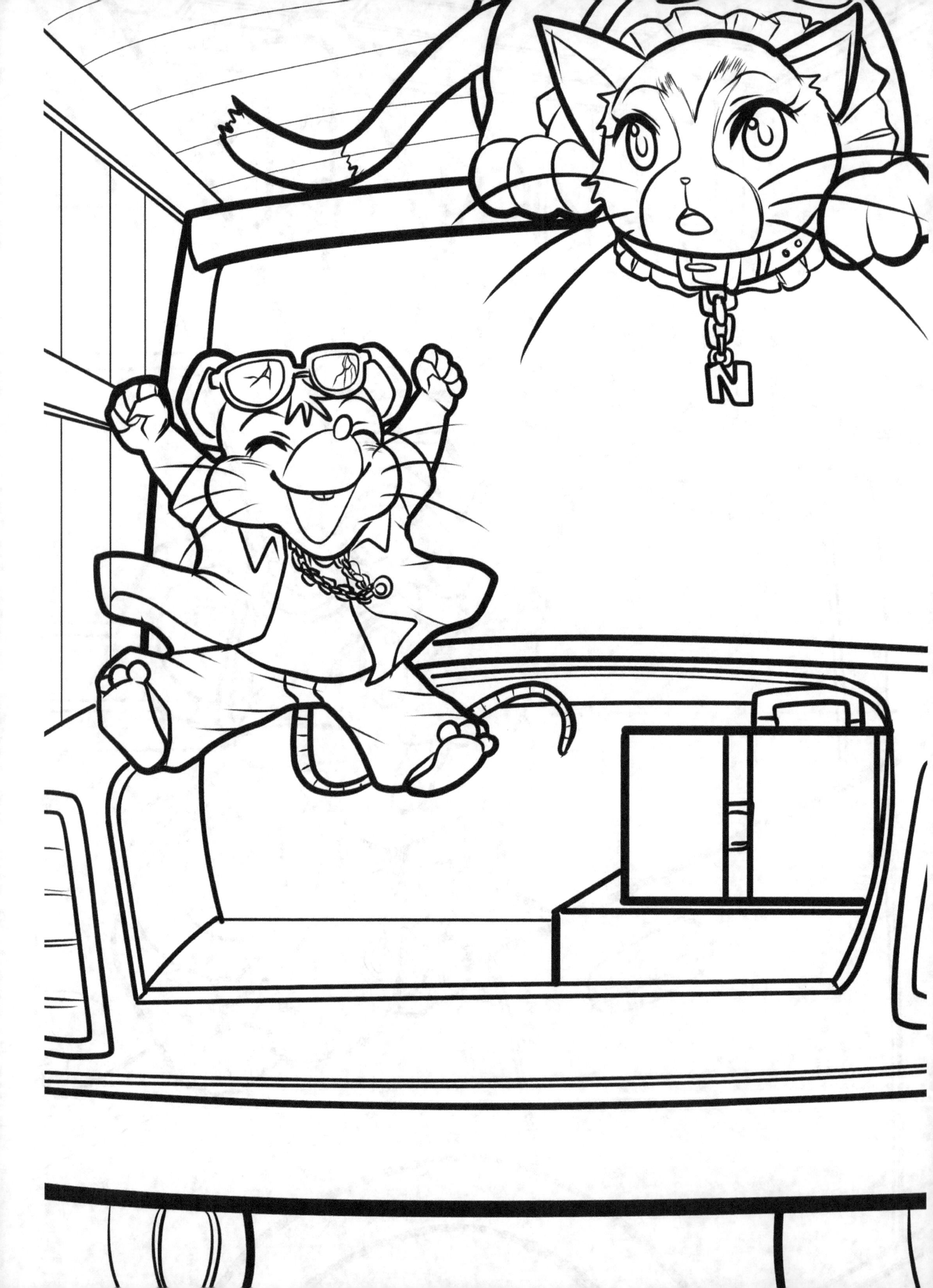

Animals Crossword

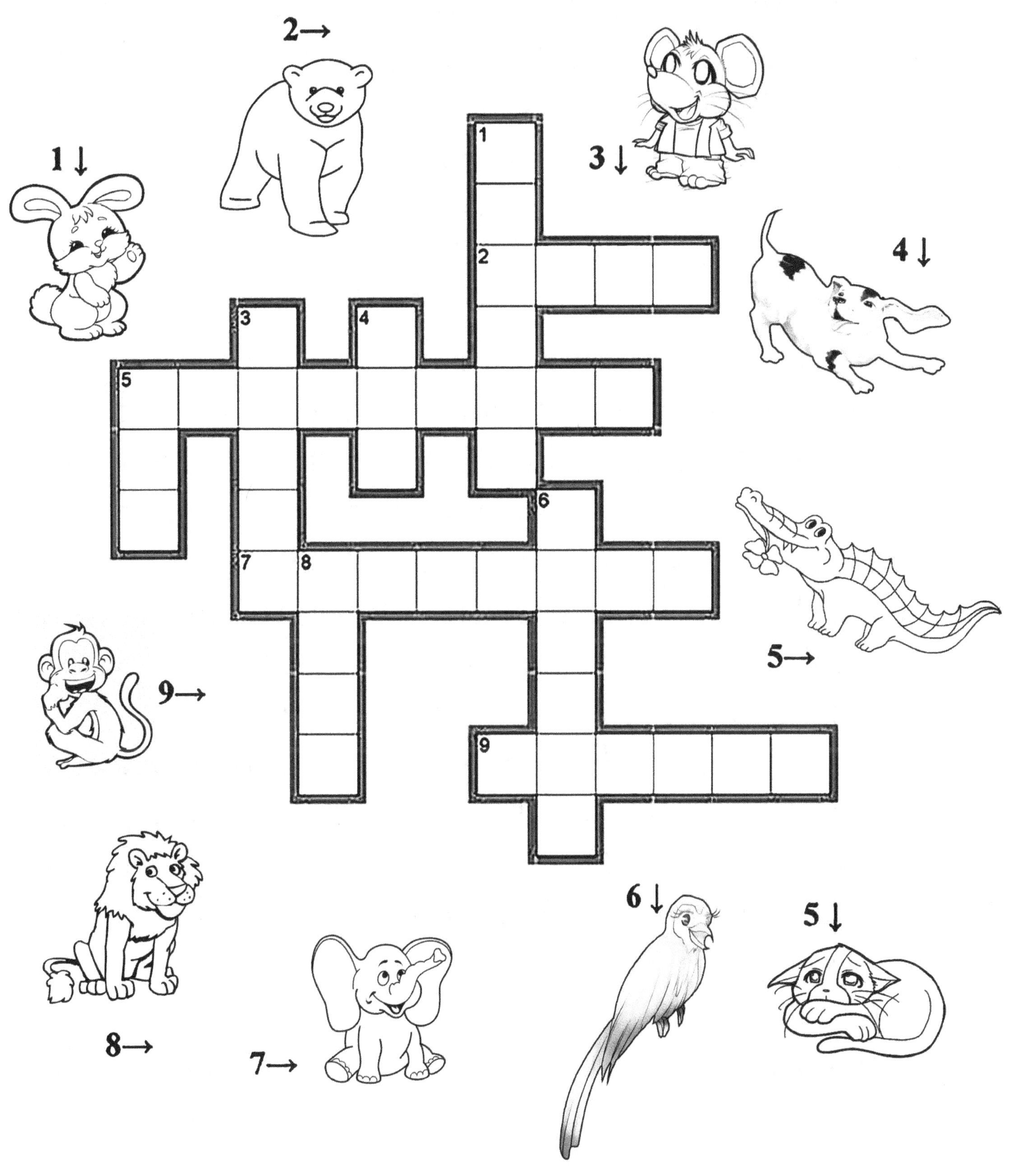

Closing Words

As the author, I faced a real dilemma: what to do with the original book, *Carlo the Mouse on Vacation*. Since this book includes four stories, which are for slightly older readers, I decided to slightly rewrite them and made these stories a part of the Carlo the Mouse series. As of right now, I have published six books about Carlo the mouse as a baby and a teen. Carlo the Mouse, Book 6 gradually connects new stories to the old stories. Chanoa, the talented illustrator, beautifully illustrated the first six books. Her illustrations are colorful, entertaining, and pleasant to the eye. All six books are available in print and as ebooks on Amazon and B&N.

The full series of adventures of Carlo the mouse will easily entertain children and grown-ups. I am planning to publish Carlo the Mouse, books 7, 8, 9 and 10, which will include *Carlo the Mouse on Vacation* adventures in 2020. As sad as I felt, I retired my first book, *Carlo the Mouse on Vacation*. I kept a few original books of *Carlo the Mouse on Vacation* for my loyal fans and me as a great reminder of how the series of Carlo the Mouse fell into my lap.

It has been some thrilling ride since I introduced Carlo the mouse to the world. Every vegetable has its time.

So does the story of Carlo the Mouse. It must find its readers, some of them far away from Florida and some of them next to my or your home. And as my young fan, Sergei, wrote in his story, may the story of Carlo the mouse never end.

I hope you had fun coloring this book and enjoyed some activities as you set out on adventures with Carlo the mouse. I would be delighted if (with their parents' permission) young artists and readers would send me their coloring pages and stories so I could see their vision too. You can scan the colored pages and then email them to olga@mrsdbooks.com. I will gladly post them on my blog at Mrs.D.Books. Have fun reading, coloring and following Carlo the Mouse!